Peter Hall's BACCHAI

The National Theatre at Work

Jonathan Croall

© Jonathan Croall 2002

Peter Hall's Bacchai is published by
NT Publications
Royal National Theatre
South Bank, London SE1 9PX
www.nationaltheatre.org.uk

Editor Lyn Haill
Designer Stephen Cummiskey
Photographs by Manuel Harlan
Drawings by Alison Chitty

Peter Hall's Bacchai is the fourth in the series 'The National
Theatre at Work'. The others are Jonathan Croall's *Hamlet
Observed* and *Inside the Molly House* and Robert Butler's
Humble Beginnings. Di Trevis' *Remembrance of Things
Proust* also covers the process of putting on a play at the
National Theatre. All are on sale exclusively at the
National's Bookshop – 020 7452 3456 or
bookshop@nationaltheatre.org.uk
Typeset in Agenda

Printed by Battley Brothers, Clapham, London SW4 OJN

ISBN No. 0 9542048-0-8

The Author

Jonathan Croall worked as an editor in book publishing and newspapers before becoming a writer and journalist. His previous books include a biography of A.S. Neill, an oral history of the Second World War, and a children's novel. He has directed and written plays for the London fringe, and now specialises in writing about theatre.

His most recent books are *Gielgud: A Theatrical Life,* and two books in the series 'The National Theatre at Work' – *Hamlet Observed* and *Inside the Molly House*. He is the editor of three magazines published by the National Theatre, *StageWrite*, *Ensemble* and *News from the National*.

Contents

Rehearsal photographs between pages 37 and 43.
Production photographs from page 67

The Cast

Bacchai
by **Euripides** in a new translation by **Colin Teevan**
with music by **Harrison Birtwistle**

Protagonists
Dionysus · Teiresias · Servant   **Greg Hicks**
Cadmus · Soldier · Herdsman   **David Ryall**
Pentheus · Agave   **William Houston**

Chorus   **Nicola Alexis**
Ewen Cummins
Lee Haven-Jones
Chuk Iwuji
Rebecca Lenkiewicz
Wendy Morgan
Richard Morris
Renzo Murrone
Stefani Pleasance
Margaret Preece
Marie-Gabrielle Rotie
Rachel Sanders
Geoffrey Streatfeild
Clare Swinburne
Jax Williams

Theban Women
Laura Anderson, Chiara Dollorenzo, Rachel Gomme, Esther Hoyuelos, Rebecca Kenyon, Styliani (Astero) Lamprinou, Emma Sweeney, Leanne Tiller

Soldiers
William R Charlton, Aidan Crowley, Elliott Fisher, David Gallagher, George Georgiou, Graeme Henderson, Ed Jaspers, Ross MacDonald, Bryce Millard, Tom Moody, Lee Rhodes, John Rogers, Joel Staley, James Williams

Director	**Peter Hall**
Designer	**Alison Chitty**
Lighting Designer	**Peter Mumford**
Movement Director	**Marie-Gabrielle Rotie**
Sound Designer	**Paul Groothuis**
Assistant Director	**Cordelia Monsey**
Company Voice Work	**Patsy Rodenburg**
Mask Maker	**Vicki Hallam**
Music Directors/keyboard/percussion	**Nikola Kodjabashia**
	Kawai Shiu
Percussion	**Martin Allen**
	Rufus Duits
Clarinet	**Alan Hacker**
Oboe	**Belinda Sykes**

Staff Director	Production Manager (*Bacchai*)
Steven Little	**Laurence Holderness**
Stage Manager	Deputy Stage Manager
Ernest Hall	**Angela Bissett**
Assistant Stage Managers	Assistant to the Designer
Gemma Bodley, Paul Greaves	**Mark Friend**
Assistant to the Lighting Designer	Deputy Production Manager (Olivier)
Danny Cunnettt	**Tom Richardson**
Deputy Production Manager (*Bacchai*)	Assistant Production Manager (*Bacchai*)
Paul Atkinson	**Tim Blazdell**
Associate Sound Designer	Assistant Voice Coach
Colin Pink	**Kate Godfrey**
Singing Captain	Costume Supervisor
Stefani Pleasance	**Carrie Bayliss**
Production Photographer	Magic Consultant
Manuel Harlan	**Paul Kieve**

Opening: Olivier Theatre 17 May 2002, before visiting Newcastle Theatre Royal from 18 to 22 June, and Epidaurus Festival, Greece, 28 and 29 June

Bacchai is part of

BARCLAYS

Olivier Theatre Season

Acknowledgements

I would like to express my deep gratitude to Peter Hall, Harrison Birtwistle, Alison Chitty, Colin Teevan and the entire *Bacchai* company, for generously allowing me to be a fly on their rehearsal-room wall, and for finding time during nine intensive weeks' work to share with me their thoughts and anxieties about the process of creating their very fine production.

I would also like to thank Lyn Haill at the National for commissioning the book and editing it with her usual care, and Lesley Bruce and Deborah Bruce for very helpfully reading it in draft.

Introduction

In March 2002 the director Peter Hall and the composer Harrison Birtwistle arrived at the National Theatre to begin rehearsing Euripides' play *Bacchai*. This book is the story of the unique act of creation which took place in the rehearsal room over the next nine weeks, during which this masterpiece of Greek classical drama, written two and a half thousand years ago, was transformed into a brilliantly imaginative piece of contemporary theatre.

The spark had been lit two years earlier, when Birtwistle sent Hall a postcard, asking: "Isn't it time we did another Greek play?" It was nearly twenty years since the two men had successfully collaborated on Hall's acclaimed production of Aeschylus' *The Oresteia,* translated by Tony Harrison, which they staged first in the Olivier theatre at the National and then in the famous open-air theatre in Epidaurus in Greece. When he read the postcard Hall, approaching seventy, knew the moment had come to fulfil a long-held dream.

For much of his life he had been haunted by Euripides' powerful and complex tragedy, and a strong desire to direct it. "I've lived with it for over fifty years, seen it three times, but never been satisfied with it. I think it's one of the most original plays ever written; I would put it in the top dozen of all time. Like Shakespeare, it's full of the most meaningful ambiguity. And whenever it's performed it seems to be extraordinarily timely."

Dissatisfied with existing translations – there are more than thirty in existence – he commissioned a fresh version from the Irish playwright Colin Teevan, who was running the drama department at Queen's University, Belfast. Teevan, who reads ancient Greek, had translated Euripides' *Iphigenia in Aulis* as *Iph...,* but had also done adapting and dramaturgical work on *Tantalus,* John Barton's ten-hour epic about the Trojan Wars, which Hall had staged recently in America and England.

His chosen designer was Alison Chitty, who had worked extensively with both him and Birtwistle. She had designed Hall's productions of Michael Tippett's opera *New Year,* and at the National his *Antony and Cleopatra.* She had also worked on Birtwistle's operas *The Mask of Orpheus, The Last Supper* and *Gawain.* All three of them had collaborated in 1988 on Hall's final productions during his time as director of the National, Shakespeare's Late Plays *Cymbeline, The Winter's Tale* and *The Tempest.*

For *Bacchai* Hall and Birtwistle enlisted as joint music directors Kawai Shiu, a Hong-Kong-born composer based in America, and Nikola Kodjabashia, a musician and composer from Macedonia, who was also an expert on Greek and Byzantine musical instruments. To complete the team Hall asked Peter Mumford to design the lighting, and Marie-Gabrielle Rotie, a dancer and specialist in the Japanese *butoh* form of dance, to work on the movement.

1. The Preliminaries

"Euripides is a great ironist, and the most eloquent of all dramatists"
— Peter Hall

Bacchai, one of Euripides' last two plays, was not performed until after his death. He wrote it when he was over seventy, having left Athens and gone into near exile in Macedonia. The story centres on the cult of Dionysus, the god of wine, music, dance, instinct and liberality.

Pentheus, a repressed and violent young man, has taken over as ruler of Thebes from his grandfather Cadmus. He and the women of the city refuse to honour Dionysus, or acknowledge that he is the son of Zeus. In revenge Dionysus, returning from the east with a band of female followers (the Chorus), sends the Theban women up the mountain to perform his wild dances. Here they join the cult of the Bacchai. Disguising himself as a priest of his own cult, he gets Pentheus, who is his cousin, to admit that he desires to see the Bacchai performing their rites. Dionysus offers to take him to the mountain if he disguises himself as a woman.

Once Pentheus arrives, Dionysus reveals his identity, and persuades the women in their ecstasy to tear Pentheus to pieces. Pentheus' mother Agave returns to the city gates with her son's head, believing in her trance-like state that it is the head of a lion. Cadmus, her father, coaxes her into understanding what she has done. The two of them are then sent into exile by Dionysus. The story explores the conflict between opposing elements in man's nature: the ordered, civilised but repressed on the one hand, the instinctive, sensual and irrational on the other. That conflict is crucially found within Pentheus himself, and leads directly to his violent death.

There are divided views on how the classics should be translated. Should you keep every word, or focus on the spirit of the original? "With drama I think you should go for the spirit, and that's what I've tried to do here," Colin Teevan says. He first did a literal translation of the Greek text, and then a version which was read at the Studio in February 2001 by a group of actors from the National. "Peter posed the question, Why are we doing this play? I then realised that the play was about the art of theatre: What is invention, what is reality, the paradox of how you see truth through artifice. So I came up with a device to frame it, based on the idea of Dionysus as the god of theatre. This is never mentioned in the text, because audiences of the time were sitting watching the play in the theatre of Dionysus, with a statue of him there, so it never had to be spelt out. But the other reason for the device was to plug a big hole near the end of the text. The equivalent of three pages are missing, where the manuscript sources have only a few fragments, and it's not clear when Dionysus makes his final entry."

Teevan revised and simplified the text, and this version was used as a basis for a three-day workshop at the National Theatre Studio in December 2001. Harrison Birtwistle set a short section of the text rhythmically, breaking down the language and showing how he intended to work. Marie-Gabrielle Rotie was also there, so Peter Hall could test out ideas about movement, which he had not used much in his earlier productions of Greek plays. "The fascinating thing about *bhuto* is that it's very actor-based, and its tempo is extremely slow. I was interested in the idea of a slow physical life and very fast speaking. I thought the contrast might work for the Chorus because everything they do, whether in words or movement, is to *tell* the audience the story."

The play appealed to him as one full of fascinating contrasts and contradictions. "It's about east and west, order and freedom, reason and emotion, faith and instinct, male and female, life and death. The task of doing the play is to balance these contradictions. This can only come from a process of work with the actors, the composer and the designer, so we build it up as we go along." He therefore decided that the music, set, masks and costumes would all evolve during rehearsals. This radical idea flew in the face of what normally happens at the National, or indeed in most other British theatres, where such elements are usually settled well in advance. Hall's stature, not least as a former director of the National, enabled him to demand and get the conditions he found most artistically congenial. As he put it before rehearsals began: "With proper theatre work, if you decide what a play is before you do it, if you decide on the route before the journey, you get nowhere. The rehearsals are to find the way."

His collaborators were fully in sympathy with his approach. Harrison Birtwistle had already worked in this way with him on *The Oresteia.* "For most of my life I sit there making decisions of which I am the lord. In the theatre it's different: you put yourself at the service of the piece, you've got to be prepared to go along with how things are while making your contribution. Peter's method means we will find things out together."

Alison Chitty too was happy with this way of working, which she and Hall had also used for *Antony and Cleopatra*. "In many ways it's very frustrating for a designer to work to the usual system, by which final designs may be demanded up to six months before the opening. It gives you much less time for reflection. For me there's no point in putting on a play if the design is finished before you start rehearsing. Apart from being incredibly insulting to the performers, that's not what it should be about. I've worked in many different ways — for example with Mike Leigh, where you start with absolutely nothing, or perhaps just a small seed somewhere. Peter's way is difficult and complicated, but it's exciting artistically."

Needless to say, some artistic decisions had been made before rehearsals began. Hall decided that the Chorus, which was conventionally either all-male (as in *The Oresteia*) or all-female (as in *Lysistrata*), should be a mixture of male and female actors, to give more tonal variety to the group of eastern women. He wanted the protagonists and the Chorus to play throughout in full masks, which he had long believed essential for coping with the extreme emotions to be found in Greek tragedy. He also decided to do the play in some form of modern dress, "so that it doesn't become antiquey".

Harrison Birtwistle had originally considered working electronically, but then decided it would be more appropriate to use percussion for his musical and rhythmical contribution to the production. He and Nikola Kodjabashia began looking for unusual instruments to achieve the sound he wanted. As with *The Oresteia*, he had one or two specially made. "Percussion can very easily be a cliché, so we're having fun finding other instruments. I think we might come up with a few surprises." Meanwhile he discussed his ideas with Kawai Shiu, and set out some provisional basic rhythms for three of the five choruses in the play.

Alison Chitty had also been busy. She brought Hall visual material to respond to, books of work by artists such as Rebecca Horne and Mark Dion whom she felt were dealing with the kind of world they were trying to create. With him she looked again at the Olivier stage, which since their collaboration on Shakespeare's Late Plays had been lifted and brought forward, and new lighting added. "It's a lovely space, but I think there's probably too much there. Peter and I are very eager to expose the theatre and make it fantastically simple. It seems the only thing you can do for *Bacchai* is to have a great disc. I started by drawing and then modelling a circular floor with a rake of 1:25. I've put it in the space to see what it looks like, and started thinking about the lighting rig."

She and Hall also talked about the location of the play, which is set between city and country. "We had to find an image of a place between places. I got caught up with this idea of something that was in construction or deconstruction, in transition. I started to think about building sites and demolition yards, and that made me think of Anselm Kiefer, whose work I really love. Then I got on to wastelands and landfill sites, which are also found between city and country. I went to a site in Croydon, with loads of flapping plastic and hundreds of birds circling round. It was strangely beautiful, more epic and weird and pagan than you can imagine."

Bacchai has eight characters, normally played – as in the National's 1972 version by Wole Soyinka, directed by Roland Joffé – by eight actors. Hall looked at various options: "I went through many contortions as to how to cast it: all men, all women, or a mixture irrespective of gender, so a man might play a woman, or a woman a man. But after the workshop at the Studio the idea emerged of using only three actors, as Euripides had done."

The idea came from Colin Teevan, who recalls its origins: "In the play Pentheus disappears from the action; he has a tragic flaw but no moment of recognition; that's taken by his mother Agave. So in a sense the two of them are one tragic character. Structurally it seemed very flawed having a new character entering with ten pages to go. That got me thinking that perhaps the same actor should play both parts. When I tried to work out how Euripides had managed to use only three actors, the structure became beautifully clear: one played the three protagonists, Dionysus, Teiresias and the Servant; another played the antagonists, Pentheus and Agave; the third played the more human, down-to-earth parts, Cadmus, the Guard and the Herdsman. Peter was convinced this was how we should do it."

Two of the actors were relatively easy for Hall to cast. "It was a great help to know I could get Greg Hicks and David Ryall, both of whom are expert in masks, and have worked with me on and off for twenty years." His other choice, William Houston, was less obvious. "Will has done no mask work, but he's a wonderful modern young actor. I saw him last year at the RSC, as Hal in

Henry IV and *Henry V*, and I thought he had a kind of passion about him that would work in *Bacchai*." A week before rehearsals began he had a brief session with the actor, introducing him to the mask.

Most productions at the National have five or six weeks' rehearsal; elsewhere in Britain three or four weeks is the norm. For *Bacchai*, Hall and his company had nine weeks. On the eve of rehearsals he reflected: "The extra time will give us the luxury of being able to discuss principles, as well as create and bring together all the component parts. But it's going to be a difficult journey."

2. Into Rehearsal

"I don't want it to be musical tourism" – Harrison Birtwistle

Monday 4 March

The company assembles in Rehearsal Room 2 at the National Theatre. Trevor Nunn, its director, greets them in the traditional manner. Members of the theatre's staff involved with the production introduce themselves to the actors. The cast then settle down to a morning's discussion of the play and its background.

Three tables are pushed into the middle of the spacious, high-roofed rehearsal room. Sitting around them are Peter Hall, Harrison Birtwistle, Greg Hicks, David Ryall, William Houston, and the 15 members of the Chorus, four of whom are trained singers. They are joined by Colin Teevan, Alison Chitty, Peter Mumford, Marie Gabrielle-Rotie, assistant director Cordelia Monsey, and staff director Steven Little. Also present is Edith Hall, an expert on ancient Greek theatre. Ernie Hall (the three Halls are not related) and his stage management team – Angela Bissett, Gemma Bodley and Paul Greaves – are positioned behind desks against the front wall.

The mood is one of expectation and uncertainty, the style informal and friendly. As usual, Christian names are used from the start. Peter kicks off with a summary of the play's themes. "*Bacchai* is about freedom, and the price you pay for it – emotionally, sexually, politically. It shows the danger of repressed emotions, but also the destruction and violence that follow when we release them. It's about everything that is in the papers every morning, but just more hideously so at the moment. During our journey over the next nine weeks we need to trust Euripides, to open up all the possibilities, to investigate and portray every extreme. The play can be evaluated in different ways; but if we deliver it as propaganda for either a belief or its antithesis we'll be betraying our audience."

He talks briefly about the use of masks in Greek drama. He suggests they enable an actor to deal with the most intense emotions and still be able to describe them to the audience. "You can't deal with violent happenings unless you control and discipline them with form." He tells the Chorus they are the centre of the play: "If we don't make you the most amazing, extraordinary cohort, we will have failed." He makes it clear they will not be speaking in unison, a method he finds too abstract and mechanical, but will share the lines individually. "However, if it works the audience shouldn't know who is speaking – which is perhaps a depressing thing to say to a group of actors!"

Harrison Birtwistle – informally known as Harry – explains how he intends to write the music, including some choral pieces, in response to what happens in rehearsals. "The Chorus will have some strong musical episodes. But I'm not writing incidental music, an emotional wash like movie music. First we need to find the rhythm of the verse, so I've already set it for three of the choruses. We have to make you into an orchestra, then once you've learnt the lines we can see where that takes us."

Next Colin Teevan fills in the background to the play. He talks about Dionysus as the god of theatre and the reason for his framing device, explaining that the original production would have been brought to the theatre of Dionysus in a procession. "*Bacchai* is Euripides' homage to theatre," he says. Edith Hall suggests that Euripides was brave to write for just three actors – earlier he had written for four or even five – but that actors at the time were used to being flexible, often having to assume several identities in one production. When Peter asks if she thinks *Bacchai* is pro-women, she replies startlingly that "the ideological content is poisonously misogynistic", and that "the moral of Greek tragedy is that unsupervised women invariably wreck things".

Marie-Gabrielle Rotie then explains the basic idea behind *butoh*, which was originally a response in Japan to the Hiroshima bomb, but is now an international dance form. She emphasises its strong interest in the unconscious, its spiritual leanings, and its use of poetic imagery. She will be taking daily early morning sessions with the Chorus, partly as warm-up, but mainly to work on a variety of movement ideas. Some she's already devised, others will emerge as rehearsals progress.

She's followed by Alison Chitty, who outlines her task of creating the world of the play using the bare essentials for a set. She explains the risk involved in leaving decisions about it until this unusually late stage. "We'll just have to understand that what we can achieve will be related to when we deliver designs. The deal is, if they can't give it to us, we don't have it. But it's amazing what can be achieved right up to the wire."

The final hour is spent talking about masks. Like Will Houston, most of the Chorus have no experience of mask work. Peter offers them some basic advice: "Approach the mask with care, discretion and pride. If you treat it with respect, it will pay you back, if you treat it as a prop it won't work. If you feel untrue in it, don't argue with it, just take it off. It must be comfortable, it must make you feel free. If you feel tense or unhappy, say so."

Greg Hicks, whose experience of mask work includes *The Oresteia, The Oedipus Plays* and *Tantalus*, talks of its positive qualities: "I found it more liberating than any other kind of work." David Ryall, who was also in *Tantalus*, endorses the stimulus the mask can provide: "Playing in a mask can inform your other work, make you much more physically aware."

In the afternoon the company starts work on the text. "It's not an ordinary read-through," Peter says. "We'll work through the play but discuss it as we go along." Much of the discussion is about meaning, with Colin providing historical clues or explanations, occasionally checking with the Greek original. One central question is, who exactly are the Chorus? Peter sees them as a group of proselytisers "like any group from abroad knocking on your door today". He stresses the importance of their foreignness, the impact of their eastern culture on the action.

As they work through, ideas about design or the use of music begin to emerge. At one point Peter says: "It might be best to let Harry loose here and create some sounds which can be recorded, and then played while Dionysus dances." He raises the question of underscoring parts of the dialogue with music or some kind of rhythm. Suggestions also come up from various people about the set: how to represent the shrine of Semele, the mother of Dionysus, or create the illusion of the earthquake that destroys Pentheus' palace.

The principal actors approach the reading in contrasting ways. David goes for understatement, delivering his lines very casually, often in a wryly comic manner, sometimes almost in a whisper. Greg is less matter of fact, picking up on mood changes, projecting his voice experimentally at different levels. Will adopts a more full-blooded approach, giving vent to full-scale anger in some of Pentheus' tougher speeches, then scaling it down for the female role of Agave.

– –

David Ryall
I don't like to get big until I've understood what I'm doing. I'm cautious
about the work until I've discovered the path to go along, I can't think of
how to say something until I know why I'm saying it. Of course it makes a
difference once you've learnt the words.

– –

William Houston
There's always that horrible moment at the read-through when you think, Do
I commit, or do I stand off? It's that whole thing about being exposed before
you're ready to be exposed. But this time I did commit, I no longer care what
people think about me, which is a big change. I've been through enough big
stuff to know that the sooner you can get rid of any feeling of being
embarrassed the better, you can then get down to work quicker.

Tuesday 5 March
The cast continue to read and discuss the play for another couple of hours.
Peter then asks them to read it again, this time without interruption. The
reading takes one hour and twenty minutes. "Terrific play," he says. "Well done,
it's going to work."

From now on the Chorus and the protagonists are to rehearse separately, until
they have become proficient enough to start integrating their work. So after
lunch, while Peter moves to a smaller rehearsal room with the principals,
Harry starts work with the Chorus, beginning with some simple rhythm
exercises. He gives each actor two claves, and gets them to try out different
rhythms, then play "pass the pulse" round a circle at different speeds. "I don't
want to talk about crotchets and quavers, I just want you to learn it," he says.
First results are ragged, but the actors soon get the hang of it, and move on to
syncopation exercises. All this is designed to attune ear and body to the
rhythms Harry has devised for their verses.

After lines have been allocated to individuals, Harry takes them through his
setting of one of the choruses, with percussionist Martin Allen providing the
drumbeat. It's an insistent, complex rhythm, full of triplets and semi-quavers,
and changes of tempo. When Kawai takes over the conducting, Harry ambles
around the room, listening as the Chorus struggle to master his rhythms. "I
promise you it gets easier," he says, and then, laconically, after an improved
rendering, "Something like that."

– –

Harrison Birtwistle
I think Peter and I have a common understanding of what we're trying to achieve. I'm not writing incidental music, that's the fundamental thing. I know what I'm looking for. I don't want to take a culture off a shelf, I want to try to find something fresh.

– –

Alison Chitty
It's a very complicated process, having a committee which thinks it can make this thing together. Actors don't normally have the privilege of being in this situation, and there's a lot of ideas floating around. I'm doing a lot of listening and smiling. I see myself as a sifter. Peter is listening and sifting too, and we'll get together later and say, Yes, a bit of this and a bit of that.

Wednesday 6 March

The rehearsal room is now arranged so that the actors can work in a circular space very similar to that in which they will eventually perform on the Olivier stage. Peter, Harry, Colin and Cordelia face them from behind a couple of desks set against the front wall. Paul, who is in charge of the script, sits on one side of them, while Ernie, Angie and Gemma are on the other. Today, one side wall of the rehearsal room is almost entirely taken up by a large mirror. A collection of brown, grey and yellow masks is lying face upwards on a table at the back. Mouths agape, eyes wide open, they make an eerie sight crowded together, with no one to animate them.

Peter explains the two schools of thought about approaching the mask: one favours the use of a mirror at the start, the other prefers working with the mask alone. He then invites the actors to try them on in the rehearsal space. "This is not a group activity, this is about you. Forget me and anyone else watching, and your colleagues. If you find a mask that gives you a charge, you can add fragments of clothing from the rail. If there's nothing there, let there be nothing. And if you simply gaze at the wall, that's all right."

Half the actors walk over to the mask table and begin to try on a mask; after a few minutes the rest join them. The reactions are strikingly varied. One actor (Rebecca Lenkiewicz) tries three masks before settling on a fourth; another (David Ryall) rejects two, then leaves the space; a third crawls under the table and briefly adopts a foetal position; a fourth remains totally still for ten minutes. Gender becomes impossible to pin down: almost everyone moves in slow motion, as if involved in a ritual. The movements are measured, graceful, sensuous: the smallest change in a hand or head position suddenly assumes significance. Some use the mirror all the time; others move inwards into a world of their own; only two, already familiar with masks (Greg, and Clare Swinburne), begin to present theirs out front. A few appear to be already carving out an identity for themselves; others seem like actors wearing a mask.

Overall Peter is encouraged: "That was a remarkable session, the level of concentration was enormous. You were very honest, and there were some beautiful things going on. One or two of you achieved a oneness between mask and body." He suggests they might have relied too much on the mirror as a safety net. "But this is just the beginning of a process; as you grow into the mask you will become social beings."

He tells them two actors withdrew from previous productions of his because of psychological problems with the mask. He then invites them to share any worries or tensions they have experienced. The Chorus actors respond in different ways. Richard Morris confesses he got a headache "trying to mould my face to the mask"; Lee Haven-Jones says he was forced to take off the first mask he tried "because of a feeling of loss"; Wendy Morgan admits "My heart was going, but I had a feeling of great power and energy"; Jax Williams says "I was anxious beforehand, but as soon as I put the mask on, I felt very liberated". Attitudes towards their fellow-actors also vary enormously: Stefani Pleasance recalls "I wanted to speak, to have a conversation", but Chuk Iwuji says "I felt I could be silent for decades."

Peter now reveals that the masks were made for two of his earlier productions, *The Oresteia* and *The Oedipus Plays*. "It was a slight cheat, I just wanted to provoke you," he explains. He now asks them to try on neutral grey rehearsal masks made by Vicki Hallam, which have been modelled on their own faces. But this time there seems no element of mystery, no real engagement with the masks, simply a buzz of conversation.

Then comes an unexpected admission from Peter. "I've made a foolish mistake. These masks are giving you nothing. My brief to Vicki was to create neutral masks, but I can see now that's a contradiction in terms. They're not charging your being at all." The actors agree, and after some deliberation it's decided that a new set of masks will have to be made..

In the afternoon Harry gives the Chorus more rhythm exercises. When they move on to chorus work Kawai takes over the conducting. His bouncing, energetic approach contrasts with Harry's more gentle, restrained but authoritative manner. As the actors gain in confidence, Harry first quietens the musicians ("Let the Chorus take the initiative") then asks them to remove the pulse ("Now they've got no security blanket"). Under his subtle coaxing the verse is taking on a shape, and the actors beginning to extract meaning as well as rhythm from the words.

– –

Greg Hicks
I'd never put a mask on before *The Oresteia*, not even at drama school. It was like finding the perfect wife. Now I can't imagine doing a Greek play without one. The mask is a doorway, through which you can get to some metaphysical world, which is very difficult to do without one. It helps me go beyond my limitations as an actor, and move into archetycal behaviour.

– –

Nicola Alexis
That session with the mask was a bit scary. Greg and Peter had talked about what we should feel, about being at one with the mask, and all that was a bit daunting. I was convinced I wouldn't feel anything, but I was wrong. I looked about a bit, then I tried one on, which I absolutely loved, so then I forced myself to try another, because I was a bit worried that I would only be able to do it with one mask.

Friday 8 March

A notice board at one side of the room is filling up with material for the company to look at. It includes histories of the *Bacchai* characters, the background to the play's original staging, and pictures and a history of the theatre at Epidaurus, which the production will visit in June. There are also newspaper articles about the conflict in Afghanistan and the Middle East. Alison has brought in a range of relevant art books to add to the growing pile on Greek myths, society and theatre, and alternative versions of *Bacchai*.

Marie is holding a movement session, encouraging the actors to control their bodies by walking slower and slower "until your batteries run down completely". The concentration and the sense of power they achieve is impressive. Afterwards Stefani takes them through a series of stretching and breathing exercises. She also introduces them to some Indonesian sounds that

might be used in one of the choruses – at Harry's request she's been
researching sounds, including war cries, from different cultures.
While Harry and the Chorus move to another rehearsal room, Peter and Colin
begin to analyse the text in detail with the three main actors. They look at the
motivation of the characters, and debate points raised by the play concerning
morality, religion, faith, myths, and much else. Several minor but important
textual changes are made to help with the rhythm or meaning of a line. Colin
restores words or phrases from his earlier draft, which both Cordelia and
assistant stage manager Paul Greaves record in their scripts.

After lunch Peter touches on the question of understudies, another element
that is normally settled in advance. Rather than have three actors covering the
three principals, he prefers to allocate the eight parts separately. Decisions
need to be made by the end of next week so Steven Little can begin working
with the relevant actors. "We'll share the parts out irrespective of gender,"
Peter says. "If anyone has a preference, let us know."

He then suggests they read through the play on their feet, with three of the
actors speaking the Chorus lines unmasked, and the rest remaining in the
space, but simply listening as women in masks. "I want to end the week by
giving people a chance to experience the play as a whole," he explains.

During this exercise the Chorus tentatively begin to produce sounds and
movements in response to the principals, who have already learnt a lot of
their lines. The unfamiliar mask work is tiring, and several of the actors
temporarily drop out of the action, and watch from the front. The running
time is a satisfactory one hour thirty-two minutes. "Good, that's thrown up a
lot that we can deal with next week," Peter says.

– –

Peter Hall
The most exciting thing about the mask is the way it releases the Chorus. I
was brought up to understand that the most complex, image-laden writing in
the Greek plays was in the choruses. If you have 15 people saying those lines
at once, if they're drilled so that they speak each syllable absolutely cleanly
and directly together, it dehumanises them, and you can't hear exactly what
they're saying. If you share out the text and have one voice speaking, with 15
masks all the same and the others *acting* but not speaking the line, you don't
know who's saying it.

3. Testing the Water

"I don't think rehearsals should be happy, I think they should be honest.
I like a certain amount of creative tension" – Peter Hall

Monday 11 March

The detailed analysis of the text has reached Pentheus' first scene. He discovers that in his absence the women of Thebes have taken to the mountains, and that his grandfather Cadmus and the blind seer Teiresias have joined the cult of Dionysus.

The actors are now on their feet, but still heavily reliant on their scripts. Peter keeps a beady eye on the correct scansion of the five beat lines (they are rarely purely iambic), tapping out the rhythm with his fingers on his desk. He also regularly reminds both principals and Chorus to emphasise the line endings. But most of the breaks in the reading are devoted to a discussion with the actors and Colin about actions and intentions.

"The real issue with Pentheus is how much he's the mob orator, how much he's in control," Peter suggests. "He's stupid, but he's also smart, and a great crowd-pleaser, with his little jokes about Cadmus. This is the politician addressing the nation reasonably, charmingly – suddenly, as he goes back into Downing Street, he's confronted by these two old men looking ludicrous, one in a fur bikini and another holding a phallic symbol!"

There's also a debate about the function of the Chorus. Peter suggests that as the representative of public opinion they are allowed to say anything. Will wonders if Pentheus, who never acknowledges their presence, actually sees or hears them, and if he does, is he aware that they are followers of Dionysus? Time is also spent exploring the nature of the characters. Is Teiresias a charlatan? What made Cadmus yield up control of the city to his unstable grandson Pentheus?

Only five pages are covered during the morning, but it's been a valuable session. The actors appear to work well with Peter's laid-back, leisurely style of direction, which involves a fruitful mixture of scholarly, practical and psychological exploration of the text. At this stage he's clearly keen to release the actors' imaginations and creativity, and to try out all kinds of ideas they put forward. The atmosphere is one of mutual trust.

After lunch, in the less cavernous rehearsal room 3, below the Olivier stage, Harry works with the four singers in the Chorus, Stefani, Richard Morris, Renzo Murrone and Margaret Preece. He gives them a brief choral piece, a first shot at introducing singing into the action. "What I don't want it to be is like an opera," he tells them.

They speak the words to get the rhythm, then sing it, first in unison, then in harmony. It's a raw, haunting snatch of song, to go near the top of the first chorus. While Kawai conducts and Nikola provides the piano accompaniment, Harry ambles round the edge of the room, listening as he goes. His notes to the singers are succinct: "I don't care much about pitch, as long as it has a shape and rhythm", and later, "In this kind of theatre there's no point in spending time on one note; the detail isn't important".

Alison Chitty's sketch for the Asian women's costumes

Back in the main rehearsal room he and Peter watch an early, rough attempt at the chorus 'Soon shall we know again', in which the women ecstatically anticipate returning to the Dionysian dance. "It's marvellously rhythmic, but I can't hear what you're saying," Peter tells them. Their second attempt is clearer: "But I could do with more exaggeration of consonants – which doesn't mean you have to be loud, just precise." He asks for a more extravagant delivery: "It's a bit reverential, a bit C of E. You're absolutely ecstatic, so the sexual tension is enormous. It's lyrical, but full of expectation. The joy needs to explode."

Harry underlines the fact that each chorus has a very different mood, and suggests to Kawai and Nikola that they try and rehearse them every day. Meanwhile he muses on whether the rhythmic pulse should begin before or on the entry of the Chorus. "I'll test my intuition rather than read the text," he tells Peter.

– –

Harrison Birtwistle
The rhythms I've set for the choruses are like an armature, a framework which you can then embellish. You have to begin with that, this is one of the rules you have to accept. The rhythm of the verse is the only way you can anchor the spoken word to music, in a one-to-one relationship. Once you've taught the actors a skeleton, using two or three beats and the rhythm, you can replace those beats with something else, even a full symphony orchestra, and it won't worry them at all. In the end the music should be very simple, it doesn't need to be complex.

– –

Kawai Shiu
Harry's music is the perfect marriage of the Apollonian and Dionysian. It embraces vigorous objectivity but sometimes it obeys nothing but pure intuition and randomness. The musical idea is as simple as can be, and yet the foreground music is as complex as any written in the last thirty years. It has the quality of obsessiveness and persistence, so it's captivating, emotionally and intellectually. Rehearsing it is a very interesting experience, although this time it's a cooperative effort, with music and drama; there's a lot of going back and forth, and that can be difficult.

– –

Nikola Kodjabashia
I'm just acting as a cyberspace orchestra, adding the mystical part of the sounds. I'm using a lot of samples, but not in a very standard way. Most of what I produce is my own idea. I'm improvising a lot, and afterwards Harry

can choose what he wants. I'm an extension of his musical imagination, and I'm happy to be that. Working with Harry is fun. It's not about intellectual bullshit, it's about life.

Tuesday 12 March

Work starts with a first attempt at plotting the Chorus' reaction to one of the play's major speeches. In the speech David as the Herdsman describes the women's wild Dionysian behaviour on the mountainside. The aim is to get the Chorus to reflect both the lyrical and the horrific elements in the story, which in turn delight and appal the Herdsman. David sits on a chair facing upstage and reads the speech to them.

The Chorus improvise moves and responses, but the effect is over-complicated. Peter warns: "The main task is to tell the story so the audience understands it. Singing, dancing, movement – all this is decoration unless it reflects the emotions and is grounded in reality. It has to come out of human intention." Meanwhile Harry is searching for the right kind of pulse to support the actors: should it be slow, should it be only intermittent. Finally he asks Colin to come up with some words of a foreign language they could use – maybe Greek or Arabic, or even something invented.

They move on to a scene between Pentheus and Dionysus. Greg improvises his moves, making use of the Chorus in imaginative ways, at one point concealing himself behind them and emerging suddenly. "Some of this will look like rubbish," he says, "but occasionally something wonderful might be glimpsed." His movement is both athletic and precise, and subtly expressive of his thought. Much of this comes from his fascination with *capoeira*, a Brazilian form of martial arts which originated in the African slave trade; in the gaps between rehearsals he's often to be found practising it in a corner.

Marie does some more movement work with the Chorus, trying with some success to recreate the "shoal of fishes" effect that Peter is looking for. Peter ponders the problem of how the movements start. "Perhaps it needs someone in charge of the Chorus, with others following a millisecond afterwards? It should be like starlings: you think they're going to separate, then they don't."

In the afternoon the actors visit the Olivier stage for the first time, for a session with Patsy Rodenburg, the National's voice coach. Bizarrely, they find themselves working on the set for the current production of *South Pacific*, with a vivid sunset projected on to the back screen. "Do you think anyone will notice if we do our show here among the palm trees?" Harry asks.

Patsy talks first about the problems they will face in the Olivier. "When you first come on this stage, you'll think you've lost your performance, because the space pulls you down. Your energy will take you to the back of the stalls, but the circle will be a problem: they'll hear you, but they won't engage with you." She then goes through a set of exercises, emphasising the importance of breathing – "with this kind of text you need to speak, think and breathe simultaneously" – and of being in a constant state of alertness on stage, which she calls "an internal tailwag". She plans to do such a session weekly, and offers individual help to any actor who wants it.

– –

William Houston
Playing both Pentheus and Agave is an interesting challenge. Is it one journey, or two characters each with their own journey? At the moment I'm thinking it's just one. But what will I be going through when Pentheus is killed, what will I do to put myself into Agave's head space? I'm concerned about the leap from one to the other. I don't know if I'm going to do something with my voice, that could sound terribly cod. At first I wondered whether I should imitate a woman's voice, but then I thought No, there should be no imitation whatsoever. Sounds must come from physicality, from what we're working on at the moment.

– –

Greg Hicks
Although I'm playing three distinctly separate characters, I feel they are all aspects of Dionysus. So the challenge is to find out how I can reverberate with Dionysus' psychic energy in all three roles. I want to make them empathetic to each other, so they have a similar flavour. After all, Teiresias the great blind prophet is Dionysus' flag-waver, while the Servant tells the story of what happens when you resist him. He tells it with a sense of terror and extraordinary wonder, which is what I've tried to work on. But in telling it I want also to get a sense of the presence of Dionysus within him.

– –

David Ryall
Cadmus and the Guard and the Herdsman are quite different people, but they have one thing in common: they're all caught up in an extraordinary situation. They're not exactly comic, but they're caught up in the comedy of life, in situations outside their normal experience. They're very ordinary

human beings. Cadmus is a pragmatist, a man who likes to think of himself as the elder statesman. The image I have is of Willie Whitelaw, dressing up in skins with a suit on, but still retaining his dignity.

Thursday 14 March

The text analysis has reached the final section of the play. Agave, still in a Dionysian trance and unaware of what she has done, enters with the head of her son Pentheus, whom she has just killed. This horrific scene is made infinitely more complex by the fact that Will is playing both mother and son.

The scene prompts further discussion about the nature of the play. "It shows what happens if you bottle up your emotions," Colin suggests. "If you don't release them normally, you'll end up doing so abnormally." Peter, as he often does, draws a modern parallel: "It's as if there were a festival celebrating cannabis for users and approvers, and it gets out of control. Dionysus is saying to the audience, you have to allow the bestial side of yourself freedom, otherwise you can destroy yourself."

The scene could easily provoke laughter, but Peter sees this as something positive. "We should go with the potential for black humour," he says. The mood remains light while they discuss how to play a particularly tricky moment, when Agave tries to piece together the bones of her son that Cadmus has brought down from the mountain. Should they be strung together, or separate? What kind of bag should they be in? Will suggests a clear plastic bag of the kind used at bomb incidents – "preferably with instructions about how to put him together".

David's concern to know the background of his character prompts a discussion with Colin of Cadmus' family history. Greg's idea of having Dionysus appear from beneath Pentheus' funeral shroud is taken up. Peter mixes comments on the verse line and the emphases with observations about the mental state of the characters as Agave and Cadmus are banished from the city.

Colin has now come up with the secret language Harry wanted for the Chorus, using plant names mentioned in the Greek original. In the final session Harry encourages the Chorus to play around with the words: high, low, fast, slow, exaggerating the consonants. "*Skullcap, Meadowsweet, Mandrake, Motherwort/ Burdock, Briony, Eyebright, Butcher's Broom...*" A language is born.

Throughout the week the acting has remained tentative. Scripts in hand, the actors are too preoccupied sorting out their intentions and changing emotions to give their lines much intensity or detailed colouring. The Chorus too are still hesitant about their words, having to concentrate first on getting the rhythm of their lines right, and learning the movements that accompany them. A formidable task is made doubly so now that they are starting to use the new rehearsal masks.

– –

Marie-Gabrielle Rotie
Because Peter is so full of ideas and energy and incredibly on fire, my role has changed from creating movement for the piece to giving little suggestions here and there. But I think the *butoh*-based training I'm giving the Chorus is helping them to tune in to each other, to be stiller, to be more receptive to the movement as a whole.

– –

Peter Hall
The Chorus has surprised me. It's not like any other in a Greek play. They don't participate directly in the action, they spend their time hiding from Pentheus, proselytising for being Bacchai, and revving up the ecstasy stakes wherever possible. It's very curious, because they don't leave the stage. Last week I began to understand that it's not a question of hiding them in a corner, but of making them participate and listen and react. They may be silent, but they're very eloquent. The other surprise, though I suppose I knew it already, is how extremely economical the play is, how beautifully crafted.

Monday 18 March
"An empty space and all of you, and me. And who am I?" The week begins with a session on the play's opening, in which Greg addresses the audience, first as himself, then as Dionysus, and finally in the disguise of one of Dionysus' priests. The question immediately arises, How, given his mask, can he make this rapid transformation clear to the audience?

Other issues are thrown up: When should the music begin? Where are the musicians to be positioned? Should they be in masks? Various solutions are discussed, then detailed work begins on the first entry of the Chorus. As eastern women the actors will eventually have saris; but for the moment they use swathes of cream material to cover their heads and bodies. The pulse starts, they slowly reveal their faces, and launch into the first chorus, 'From Phrygia, from Lydia, I followed Dionysus' drum.' It's a powerful moment.

The actors now seem more confident with the words and rhythms, but the physical and verbal expression is still very erratic and uncertain. "Subtext or pastel acting doesn't work, you have to be external, like a very good caricature," Peter tells them. "You have to show attitude, it needs to be primary colours. Unless we get to a high pitch you won't get that colour. I'm interested in slow, concentrated movement full of huge emotions. The image is of water on the point of boiling."

In conjunction with Colin he spells out the shifts of meaning from one section of the chorus to the next. He wants more tonal differences, and reminds the actors to give an upward inflection to the end of each line. "Don't worry about over-acting, I'll tell you if you need to modify it." The actors go through the chorus again, with noticeably greater drive and coherence.

Later Harry rehearses the second chorus, 'Hear this, Demeter, goddess of the cornfield', with its mixture of frenzy and lyricism. Here the actors are finding it hard to get his complex rhythms right. "With the off-beat sentences there's always more time than you think," he tells them. "Don't be anxious, lie back on it, make it more cool." It's a fruitful hour that moves the work up a significant notch. Harry has now set all five choruses, of which four are developing power and precision.

— —

Chuk Iwuji
For the Chorus, learning all the different ingredients is very difficult. There's so much to think about before you even utter one line. Before you start thinking about intentions you've got to think about what your body's doing, in relation to yourself and to other people. Then you have the rhythm and the music. But the good thing is that with all these disciplines you know when you're doing it wrong. There's nowhere to hide.

— —

Richard Morris
It's very weird having to look out front such a lot, I'm not sure how I'll get on with that. It also takes a while to get to grips with how much you should do with your body, how much movement is extraneous: as a singer I'm used to doing large, histrionic gestures on big stages. Normally I use my face a lot, so it feels strange not having to do so. You also feel very alone in the mask.

Wednesday 20 March

The actors are beginning to discard their scripts as the detailed blocking and interpreting of the text continues. This morning they've reached the scene where David as the Guard brings the disguised Dionysus in to Pentheus as a prisoner.

David, in a modern flat cap, is trying to pin down his character. "Did you want me to do my American soldier guarding suspected terrorists at Guatemala Bay?" Peter: "No, I didn't." Instead we get a gentle, working-class guard with a North Oxfordhsire burr. Peter builds on David's idea: "Perhaps you come in tough, but then show another side. You're telling Pentheus that the priest seems harmless; he's someone you might want to have a drink with at the bar. Someone who is a bit of a mystery."

They move on to the first *stichomythia*, the word used in Greek drama for a scene involving the rapid interchange of one-line speeches between two characters. Harry has introduced a quiet drum pulse which Will and Greg speak over. This additional element at first proves tricky to handle. At one point Will suggests a gear-change is needed. "No, let's just take it a step at a time," Peter says. "This is the structure, we can colour it later."

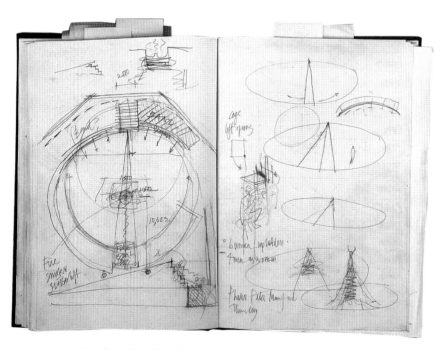

Pages from Alison Chitty's notebook

Alison and Peter have been refining ideas about the set, which is now minimal. Gone are many of the original ideas, such as Semele's shrine, city gates, a river running across the stage. Alison is still experimenting with ideas about the route to the mountain. Her first idea was to have ladders for the women to climb, another involved scaffolding, but both have proved too mechanical to let the audience's imagination work.

After spending a sleepless night thinking about the set, Peter has made another radical change: "I've decided to turn the whole thing round. The city is now the auditorium, the stage is the no-man's land where the city ends and the wild begins, and the wild is backstage – which will be fine at Epidaurus, because there will be 40 miles of Greek landscape there. But it will also work in the Olivier."

Harry has asked Stefani to teach the Chorus *sprechstimmer*, a form of delivery which is half speaking and half singing. But after experimenting with it he has decided it's not the sound he wants. Meanwhile he's been finding other sounds from unexpected sources. Having created one on his radiator at home, he's asked the workshop to fashion him a length of wire caging so he can re-create it in the rehearsal room. He's also persuaded the sound department to record the noise of a trolley being rolled along the corridor outside the rehearsal room. It sounds like a huge drum.

Meanwhile a crisis is brewing amongst the four singers. As yet they have only been given one choral piece, and even that has been swiftly rejected by both Harry and Peter as being too operatic. "I haven't found a world for them yet, and they're getting a bit angry," Harry admits. "They're saying, What am I doing here?"

– –

Alison Chitty
A lot of the set changes have come out of the rehearsals. Usually this kind of evolution happens in the studio, but now it's just happening in public. Certain things became an encumbrance or difficult to manoeuvre, or restricted the way Peter could use the space. I'm a great one for restraint and expressing things simply, so I was happy to go along that road. The earlier version was more poetic, more evocative, I loved the way it was a contemporary no-man's land. I'm sorry to see it go – but I've got it up my sleeve for another time.

Thursday 21 March
In one of the dressing rooms Alison, Vicki and costume supervisor Carrie Bayliss are trying out the new rehearsal masks on each actor in turn. The difference from the previous ones is striking: the masks are now painted with bold, exaggerated features, and their mouths have been widened, giving them more character.

Jax is the first to be called, to have her mask fitted in front of the mirror. She feels it's too close to her eyes for comfort, and Vicki adjusts it to give her more freedom. That done, Alison says: "If we ask you to take your clothes off, are there any limits to what you're prepared to show?" She marks Jax's answers on a checklist.

Lee is next to arrive. "Lovely, it's off the face," he says, as Vicky ties on the cream band that fixes the mask to his head. Carrie then gives him a blood-red sari-type wrap to wear. "If you think it's hard learning lines, just wait until you have to deal with saris," Alison observes. Asked about exposing parts of his body, Lee says he is happy to be "bollock naked" if necessary.

Mask-making is a complicated process involving several stages, starting with taking a face cast of the actor, and ending with the painting of the mask. Because of the large number required for *Bacchai*, Vicki has brought her models in to the National and is making rubber moulds with the help of the props department. "In an ideal world the actors would have their performance masks earlier than this," she says. "But in this case we've had to spend five or six weeks on rehearsal masks, so that's not been possible."

After lunch the company rehearses the 'Soon shall we know again' chorus. All the actors are now equipped with rehearsal masks and red saris. As they put them on and prepare to start, the room falls silent. The visual effect is stunning, and Peter discreetly records it with his miniature digital camera. Having mask and costume clearly helps the actors, who give the chorus a new vigour and clarity. "That was remarkably good, the text was amazingly clear," Peter says. "The masks really enhanced your speaking. The exciting thing for me is that it vindicated the idea of one person saying a line clearly on behalf of all of you. The magic of the mask is working, the groups you made couldn't have been more beautiful if a choreographer had designed them."

However, a rehearsal of the opening chorus proves less effective. The balance with the percussion is wrong, Peter says he can't understand the words, Harry feels the actors are confusing energy with loudness, and Marie suggests there are too many hand movements going on. Peter asks them to be more physically aware, to take movements off each other, and not to lose the power of the mask by drooping their heads.

Much work remains to be done. Yet this has clearly been a breakthrough session for the Chorus. Apart from Marie, none of the actors is a trained dancer, yet the physical and aesthetic demands being made on their bodies are considerable, even before the complication of wearing masks is added. In the circumstances their progress in just three weeks is remarkable.

— —

Harrison Birtwistle
The pulse we've put in under the *stichomythia* isn't easy for the actors. They can understand it technically, but when they start acting it begins to rock a bit, you have to constantly bring them back to it. The problem is that they don't have any technical procedures to understand it. If I say to the musicians you're half a beat late, they know what I'm talking about. But you can't say that to actors. They feel they should speed it up, not realising that isn't the answer, that it's actually a question of putting more energy into it.

— —

Peter Hall
Harry is more or less making up the music as we go along, and adjusting it where necessary. It's very harsh, very barbaric, very rhythmic; when it operates at its best it helps clarify the text and sustain the mood. One does have a strange cosmic feeling of what it was like when Monteverdi started inventing opera, with just half a dozen musicians and six singers improvising for six months — until the accountants moved in and said, Wouldn't it be better if the composer wrote it all down beforehand and the singers learnt it and then you rehearsed it — and the Venetian opera was born.

4. Moving On

"At the moment I'm writing speculative music" – Harrison Birtwistle

Monday 25 March

The Chorus and protagonists work together for the first time on the recognition scene, when Agave discovers she has killed her own son. Will now has the required prop: a wild-eyed, blood-soaked head of Pentheus, its face modelled on his own.

Peter teases out the mood of 'Dance to the drumbeat', the final chorus which prefaces the arrival of Agave from the mountain. "It's one of the most grotesque scenes in all drama," he suggests. "I think the Chorus' attitude is, God, how horrible – but I love it. You're not yet hostile, you don't realise until afterwards the moral implications, that you've joined a religion that ends in cannibalism and infanticide. You are insisting you are right when you half-know you are wrong."

David and Will wrestle with Cadmus' efforts to make Agave recognise the terrible deed she has done. "I'm trying to find my reality, but at the moment I'm not sure where I am," David admits. "It's almost like he's telling her a bedtime story so she won't go crazy." Peter agrees, and draws another modern parallel: "It's the therapist saying, Tell me what you see, give it to me in your own words." They go back to simply reading the scene, to help them pin down the exact timing of Agave's awakening. Soon it begins to run more effectively.

In the afternoon Peter calls for a run-through of the last third of the play, in masks. "Don't worry if things fall apart, but really work us as if we were the audience." The actors are now mostly off the book, and are able to get through it with only a couple of interruptions. "We're getting there, it will work," Peter says. "But it needs lots more consonants from the Chorus, lots more narrative energy. It's not enough to say a line, you have to pull it through the mask to get the clarity. We also need more disciplined movement. I always knew who was speaking, because you were the only one reacting to the line you were saying. *Everyone* must act every line, although in a very controlled and minimalist way.

David then has to leave early because of another commitment. Rehearsals are frequently disrupted in this way because a few of the actors are in other shows in London. David is playing Gloucester in the Almeida production of *King Lear,* while Greg is Brutus in the RSC *Julius Caesar* at the Barbican; both are doing eight shows a week on top of the *Bacchai* rehearsals. The Chorus is also affected: Chuk too is in *Julius Caesar* but also the RSC *Hamlet*, while Clare is appearing in Peter's production of *Lady Windermere's Fan* at the Haymarket. Apart from the physical demands this places on the actors, it means they have to miss rehearsals on matinee days, and leave early on other days to comply with Equity rules on working hours. However, careful planning of the use of rehearsal time is helping to keep disruption to a minimum.

— —

Lee Haven-Jones
Being in a mask is an intensely lonely experience. It just feels as if you're a pair of eyes on legs, because you can't see your limbs. It's a profound experience, almost like being locked up in prison. As an actor you're trained to be physically aware, but if you can't see your body, it's very difficult to know what you're doing. When you take a mask off after running a bit of the play, the sense of release is profound.

— —

Rachel Sanders
The movement is very difficult: as soon as you put on the mask it all changes, you have no idea what you look like. If you're at the front you have no idea what's going on behind you, and you can't look at other people. It would be useful if individually we were able to go out front and watch what we're doing.

Wednesday 27 March
Peter, Alison and Carrie – with Marie and Cordelia also in attendance – spend the morning in rehearsal room 3, discussing their costumes in turn with the three principals. Alison's aim is to gather in people's ideas, sift them, and come back with firm suggestions. As a stimulus she passes round her rough costume sketches, and photographs of faces that have suggested the characters to her. The ideas flow thick and fast on all sides.

Greg
Dionysus' priest. A luscious young man, maybe only 18? Think of Jim Morrison, or Bowie as Ziggy Stardust. Long blond locks – maybe dreadlocks. Trousers

that link with Asian culture. An animal belt perhaps. But how to create the bull's-head mask?

Teiresias. Not a crouched old man. More of a long thin mystic. Christopher Lee in *Lord of the Rings*? He's only just joined the cult, so his skins are new. Probably upper class. Plastic grapes and vine leaves on head; he and Cadmus as terrible tourists?

Servant. Pure and honest. Straight and faithful. A kind of valet or batman. The kind of man Pentheus would like. Naïve, jailbait. A mask with compassion in it.

David

Cadmus. A politician, a man of some solidity. A mask with dignity. Perhaps tailored military shorts, long socks. Possibly panama and plastic flowers. Medals? Probably cravat rather than jacket.

Herdsman. He's impressed by the new god, then spooked. Drawing too rural Wiltshire – needs toughening up. Bearded? Definitely stubble.

Guard. An NCO, perhaps 35? Very efficient soldier. Very physical. Uniform.

Will

Pentheus. Bisexual, but not camp – more ambiguous. Luminously attractive. Suit or military uniform? Uniform, but pale silvery grey, very chic. Shades? No, will get a laugh. Maybe summer gear. Off-white coat, medals, brass buttons. Probably a collar and tie man.

Agave. As feminine as possible. Breasts – or just a softening of Will's contours? Expensive lingerie, silk stockings – but wrecked and bloody from the hunt.

It's been a fruitful brainstorming session, giving Alison plenty to sift.

"Are we putting too many ingredients in the stew?" Peter asks Harry after lunch. He suggests spending the afternoon working out the "journey" of the choruses, then working on each, first only physically, then only vocally. But Harry argues that the actors need more of a vocabulary before they can do that; for example, they might want to create sounds. He's also aware that he urgently needs to come up with material for the singers.

Peter readily gives way, and Harry and the Chorus show him a sample of the sounds they've already created for 'Soon shall we know again'. With Kawai conducting, they demonstrate their repertoire of clicks and drones, which provide more of a "foreign" flavour to the verse. Richard enhances it by improvising the sound of a didgeridoo-style instrument; Harry walks around the space, listening and adding some emphatic grunts of his own.

"This is the way to go," Peter says. "All this helps us to understand the words more clearly."

– –

Harrison Birtwistle
One problem is that Peter wants each chorus to have an energy going right through it. But you've got to have space for music, so I have to encourage him to leave gaps. Music creates something else, it gives you time for reflection. If you have an image like 'sweet river', the music can illuminate the image.

Thursday 28 March

With Easter looming – tomorrow is Good Friday – Peter calls for a first complete run-through. Inevitably the actors are not yet totally sure of their lines, and the success of the work varies from scene to scene. But new qualities are emerging.

The Chorus and the protagonists are more engaged with each other's words and actions. Greg's physical dexterity is apparent, and he delivers the description of Pentheus' death with immense vocal skill. David is finding some blackly comic elements within the action, and beginning to unleash the power he has so far kept hidden. Will is reining in his anger as Pentheus, so giving it more subtlety, while also finding the character's bisexuality.

As he has up to now, Peter keeps his eyes more on the text than on the action in front of him, marking his script where he spots wrong emphases, downward inflections, broken lines or faulty rhythm. As a director who admits he hears more keenly than he sees, this technique reflects his concern to nail down the story with absolute precision and maximum clarity. Yet he also finds time to notice things that are going wrong in visual terms.

The run takes one hour fifty minutes, twenty minutes over Peter's target length. "Thanks for your bravery, it was very valuable to get a sense of the overall shape," he says at the end. After giving notes to the principals he turns to the Chorus. "You're doing a fantastic job. What it needs now is thinking through emotionally. We *have* to know clearly the Chorus' emotional state as it begins and ends a chorus. At the moment that's even more important than the physical line. The parts that go wrong are the parts that we haven't built properly. We just need to keep our nerve until we get the details right. Some of the masks have acoustic problems, with others it's just a question of consonants. The Greek Chorus hardly ever works on stage, but this one's going to. It's very exciting. So please learn the text by next week, and have a good Easter."

— —

Greg Hicks
I like to freefall in rehearsal, to have the freedom to explore, to do the A-Z of activity. Peter is a most remarkable example of someone who doesn't like nailing anything down until he thinks it's pretty nearly what we want. So he trusts us to explore and inquire in our own way, while he monitors us. He gives us freedom to go right to the limits. Conversely he's utterly specific, and his sensitivity to the weight of language is just breathtaking.

— —

David Ryall
You can get very bothered by Peter's preoccupation with the text. But I do understand it, so I don't rebel against it, I try to work with it, because my ear isn't necessarily right. He has such a huge understanding of plays, acting, performance, he doesn't miss a trick, and he doesn't miss what's important. He can also be very down to earth, which I like.

— —

William Houston
I'm aware that if I pay Peter too much respect, if our relationship becomes one of child-parent or student-teacher, that's not necessarily a good thing. I like to work with conflict in rehearsal, you can save a lot of time. At the moment we're setting down our roots and sorting out our relationship. He keeps saying to me, I'm trying to work out how you are as an actor, which is a very lovely way of saying, Do what you want to do.

— —

Cordelia Monsey
Peter has an uncanny ear for rhythms and stresses, and drives actors bonkers in the early stages of rehearsals. But once they accept his demands, they come to realise that he has taught them how to express with perfect precision the thought they want to convey.

Tuesday 2 April

Rehearsal room 3. Peter and Harry, with Colin and Cordelia also present, work jointly with Greg and Will on the second scene between Pentheus and the disguised Dionysus. The actors are now off the book, and are noticeably sharper on both the meaning and the rhythm of the verse.

Some of the words in the *stycomythia* have been changed to make the rhyming more overt. But the actors are struggling to tie the words and rhythm into the pulse. Will says: "If we finish off the pulse, I feel I have to wait, and that goes against the grain of what's on the page." Peter reassures him: "Waiting is fine, the pulse allows you to take time." Harry chips in: "You should keep the words relating to the beat, but the stress can be like natural speech, rather than too close to the pulse. That's the essence of syncopation." He beats out the rhythm of a few bars from Stravinsky's *The Rite of Spring* to demonstrate.

They go on to explore a turning-point in the scene, the radical shift from confrontation to intimacy when Pentheus admits he wishes to see the Bacchai in their savage state on the mountain. Will feels this may be a sexual moment with Dionysus, and Greg suggests they physicalise it. They try it this way, but Peter is uncertain: "Physical contact may help us along the way, but we may end up not using it."

They move on to the Herdsman's speech describing the Bacchai's wild activities on the mountainside. Peter and David explore the text in detail, charting the change from lyricism to horror. Peter offers an insight into one trait in the man's character: "He's a simple herdsman, he went to the village school, and he's interested in words." Colin observes: "What he's skirting round is the fact that they're all stark naked at seven in the morning."

After lunch it's back to work on the choruses. The musicians, Alan Hacker, Belinda Sykes and Rufus Duits, have arrived. Alan, who's worked often with Harry since their student days together, plays the sopraninno saxophone and a basset clarinet that he's restored. Belinda is on oboe, but is also in charge of a range of other instruments, some of them hers, others ones that Harry and Nikola have found. Among them are an alto *shawm*, a kind of ethnic oboe, a large shawm called a *zurla*, a big bamboo flute, and a soft shawm called a *duduk*. Rufus, a Cambridge postgraduate student, joins Martin on percussion, which includes Japanese and Macedonian drums, blocks and cow bells. With Kawai at the conductor's chair, one corner of the room is now specifically their area, but shortage of space means that a platform has had to be erected above it, to house Nikola and the synthesiser on which he is creating his samples. ("I am the temporary god," he says from on high.)

Bursts of sound – wild, lyrical, sensuous – now punctuate or introduce the choruses, and give them a marked boost in energy. Clare asks if the Chorus can improvise on some of the lines; the result opens out the action and creates some interesting shapes. Marie works to get more variety in the movement, sometimes moving as part of the Chorus, sometimes watching and offering ideas from out front.

As they consider what kind of dance the women might do Peter, whose adrenalin is now going at full bore, takes off his jacket and gets into the thick of it. Absorbed with the exploration, light on his feet, he suddenly seems startlingly youthful. He and Marie feed off each other's ideas. At the end of the afternoon he says: "The *bhuto* work is wonderful, but it needs to be offset by other types of movement." Marie agrees: "It's good for listening and the slow pulse, but for raw emotion you need something else."

> – –
>
> *Nikola Kodjabashia*
> Harry is very familiar with unusual percussion instruments, but we have to be careful about not sounding ethnic, because everything in the production is very stylised.

> – –
>
> *Colin Teevan*
> This way of working could be very stressful, when you've got no idea of the end-product, and four or five different basic pulls on it. But because we're agreed the text is the basis, those pulls can work.

> – –
>
> *Geoffrey Streatfeild*
> One problem in the Chorus is that we're getting everything at once - the initial blocking, our polishing up notes, our line readings, our musical notes, our initial movement and then the polishing of it – but then we don't repeat it. Quite often we're given something very specific, and we know we can do it, but not until we're another three weeks down the line.

Thursday 4 April

The Chorus are working without the musicians, who are rehearsing elsewhere. With Marie and Peter they're working on the chorus 'Hear this, Demeter'. Peter

— who confesses that his definition of paradise is to be always rehearsing —
has pitched himself into the space again, trying to make the beginning and end
more precise, and to ensure that the movement is not too fast. "Bear in mind
the image of heavy oil," he suggests. After a hard but fruitful session the goal
is achieved. "That was really terrific, visually very clear and interesting. The
most magical things happened when you were tight together." To Marie he
says: "I've messed you around, we've changed it so many times." Marie seems
unworried: "I don't feel any ownership, it's a collaborative thing."

The actors then move to the Olivier stage, for a mike rehearsal. Peter
emphasises that microphones are not being worn to amplify the actors'
voices, but to give them a greater resonance, and to remove the "boxy"
sound you can get with a mask. Paul Groothuis, the production's sound
designer, explains how best to achieve clarity while wearing a mask with a
mike in its nose. "If you start shouting it will be uncomfortable, it will vibrate
in your head," he says. "Try it out in the auditorium; you won't get it right
straight away."

Peter and Harry sit in the middle of the stalls, with the actors dotted around
them. Peter tells him: "What excited me about *The Oedipus Plays* was that the
resonance that Paul achieved then made it seem like the mask was speaking."
They watch and listen as the actors take turns to speak lines from the play
from the stage. Ewen Cummins from the Chorus is first, then Will, wearing a
mask for the first time. Paul and his team experiment with sound levels, and
demonstrate the difference between an amplified and unamplified voice.
Peter stresses yet again the need to keep the mask presenting out front:
"Think of your mask as a magnet to the audience, while your body can move
freely." Harry is concerned that when the actors move, the sound doesn't seem
to travel with them.

Back in the rehearsal room after lunch, Alison and Carrie talk with Peter and
the Chorus about the women's costumes. The discussion touches on caked
mud, jewellery, dreadlocks, and the saris, which have now been reduced in size
— Alison offers a lightning demonstration of how to put them on and take
them off. The animal skins are proving a problem; Carrie is still searching for
the appropriate material. Peter warns of the difficulty: "It's something that's
littered with cliché and vulgarity. But the dialectic between animal and human
skin is important. The women are wearing these skins because as Bacchai
they're in touch with nature. It mustn't be saucy or titillating." Alison promises

to absorb all the comments and questions, and organise fittings very soon. The production is shaping up well. Peter and Harry, who clearly have enormous respect for each other's skills and vision, see eye to eye a good deal of the time – on what needs fixing, on what doesn't fit in with the style of the production. Where they differ, the matter is talked through and resolved without difficulty: there are no artistic temperaments on view.

On practical matters solid progress is being made. Costume fittings are starting to punctuate rehearsals, and the set is now finalised – the path to the mountain is to be a diagonal walkway at the back of the stage. Meanwhile Alison and Vicki continue to work on the masks to be used in performance.

– –

Carrie Bayliss
The Asian women have been the main challenge with the costumes. We still haven't found the right material for the animal skins. They work well when you put them over modern clothes such as those that Teiresias and Cadmus are wearing, but over naked bodies it's more of a problem. We may end up using something like leather.

– –

Peter Hall
I have no idea whether the production is going to work, you never do at this stage. But I know absolutely where I am going and what I am doing. I'm not worried about finding it, because I've found it. I can't exactly explain what it is, but I know when I don't have it. Doing Greek plays is rather like Chinese cooking: it takes ages to chop up the little bits, but once you put it all together it all happens very fast. The choruses are very hard to learn, but I'm delighted with the talent and dedication of this group. It's always a problem with masks, you can't design them until you know what you're doing, and you can't know what you're doing until you've got the masks. It's a vicious circle. But with the set now just an empty stage and a lighting rig, I think we've got the metaphor right

William Houston and Greg Hicks in rehearsal

Richard Morris, Rachel Sanders, Nicola Alexis, Peter Hall, Wendy Morgan, Lee Haven-Jones, Geoffrey Streatfeild, Jax Williams

Top: Peter Hall and Alison Chitty

Above: Lee Haven-Jones, Marie-Gabrielle Rotie, Jax Williams

PHOTOGRAPHS BY MANUEL HARLAN

Rebecca Lenkiewicz, Clare Swinburne, Margaret Preece, Geoffey Streatfeild, Jax Williams, Rachel Sanders, Lee -Haven-Jones, Ewen Cummins, Renzo Murrone, Chuk Iwuji, Nicola Alexis, Marie-Gabrielle Rotie

William Houston, Greg Hicks and Marie-Gabrielle Rotie

David Ryall

Top: Lee Haven-Jones, Renzo Murrone, Ewen Cummins, Nicola Alexis, Stefani Pleasance and Wendy Morgan

Above: Harrison Birtwistle, Colin Teevan and Peter Hall

5. Changing Gear

"This is how theatre should always be, but very rarely is" – Peter Hall

Tuesday 9 April

A movement session with traces of *bhuto* to start the day. Marie works with the Chorus: each chooses an animal, then creates its movements at minimal speed. Some are lithe and graceful, others full of contained power.

On to the 'Hear this, Demeter' chorus. "Search out the antitheses," Peter exhorts the actors. "And use the searchlight of the mask on the audience." The Chorus are now hearing the music for this section for the first time; the actors sit on the floor and work on absorbing the new element. The music is sinuous, flowing, questioning. Harry wonders if it's too long.

They do it on their feet, with a lot of punch. But Peter's not satisfied. "It's a bit abstract, a bit poetic. We need different voices, coming from your heart. Personalise it, it needs more anguish, more desperation. It's all a bit Third Programme." Twice more, and his thoughts are becoming deeds.

In the afternoon there's a progress meeting in the props office, attended by Alison, the assistant designer Mark Friend, production manager Laurence Holderness, assistant stage manager Gemma Bodley, and members of the props department. Alison lists the items that have recently been cut, and promises to have the final set model and costume drawings ready tomorrow. Discussions centre on getting the right kind of ivy, making the sacred shafts properly phallic, and how much to spend on fake sub-machine guns. There's also a serious debate about Pentheus' body, which needs to be completely reassembled. It's decided to buy a complete plastic skeleton, and separate the parts into "various forms of gore".

Paul Wanklin, a pyrotechnic expert and the National's senior armourer, offers alternative suggestions for the fire that burns down Semele's tomb, and it's decided to lay on a demonstration for Peter. An hour later in the metal work-shop he's shown various options, including a six-foot column of flame, and approves one which will entail fire running along a channel across the stage.

– –
Marie-Gabrielle Rotie
All my original conversations with Peter were about trying to find a counterpoint between slow-motion movement and the normal speed of text. But we agreed that it didn't work. It's not that the *butoh* has been thrown out, because it's about more than just being slow; but it's meant a whole dynamic change. One of the problems is that the movement always has to be big and out. So the *butoh* has to take a slightly back seat, because it's more internal.

Thursday 11 April
Harry is continuing to compose his "speculative" music on the hoof. His method is to try out various phrases with the musicians, which he then writes down and puts in a ring binder. At the end of the day he selects what he thinks works best, and Kawai notates and sometimes transcribes the music using a computer, then pastes the sheets alongside the text for the musicians, so creating a score.

Work has reached the 'Go you hounds of Hecate' chorus. "You should aim for complete ugliness," Peter says. He decides to have the Chorus imagine the killing of Pentheus as they tell it, with Jax and Lee miming mother and son. He sets it from within the Chorus, throwing himself into the action, contorting his body to show what he's after. ("God, I wish he was my granddad," one of the Chorus whispers.)

Greg, now playing the Servant of Pentheus, tackles the ten-minute speech in which he describes his master's death. The effect is mesmerising: he builds the story with clever changes of pace and pitch, using his body with deft economy, and drawing in the Chorus, who respond imaginatively. "Marvellous, you got an extraordinary cohesiveness," Peter remarks.

Later they work again on the complex Agave recognition scene. Pentheus' blood-stained head on the pole is now masked, to fit the style of the production. Peter urges Will and David to keep the scene light, but they become bogged down in analysing it. "I think we're spending too much time naturalistically," Peter says. "Now we've started to pick at it, it becomes full of problems, which it wasn't before. If we strike a note of self-pity, we're lost. The temptation to get emotional is huge for both of you, but the scene is wonderful if you play it simple and stoic."

– –
Greg Hicks
In this kind of play you're asked to give the whole of your body, so I'm doing more physical work than I would normally do. It's important to be in a constant state of readiness, a bit like a pilot waiting for the all-clear to take off. If I sit down for an hour, I can't just get up and do it, my body has to be alive and alert.

– –
William Houston
The recognition scene is a terribly difficult scene. We were pulling it apart too much, but sometimes you have to do that. It's like the princess and the pea, you know there's a pea somewhere, and you've got to find it. Something wasn't right. I think part of the problem is that Agave and Cadmus are in such different places psychologically.

Friday 12 April
A few minutes to go before another run-through begins. This time designers and the production team have joined the onlookers. Tension is in the air. Greg is practising his *capoeira* in one corner, Marie flexing her limbs in another. An oboe echoes mournfully in the background. Around the edge of the room the Chorus find different ways to relax: massage, yoga, handstands, reading.

The run holds together well: the Chorus have a lot of power and energy, and the main narrative speeches are telling the story clearly. David's Guard character is now emerging with an edge of humour, and Will is clearly settling in to his mask and showing his profile much less. Peter calls it a good beginning. "You had tremendous commitment and concentration."

He then outlines the problems: the movement is too fussy, the start and ends of choruses are not well enough defined. He's also worried that the band – he calls them Harry and his Hot Four – are playing too loudly, and drowning many of the words. Harry acknowledges the problem, and promises they will lower the volume later. He himself feels the Chorus is more secure now, but starting up is still a problem: "I can see you thinking, Hell, I've got to do it now; but all you have to do is relax, there's always more time than you think."

The run took two hours. Peter still wants twenty minutes off that length. "I'll take out some of my pauses," Greg says.

– –

Peter Hall
There's a hell of a lot to do with Harry, to make the musical texture even
more complex and richer. Fortunately, we're working with a geniius. I know
I've got to persuade Will to play more delicately and more lightly, more
ironically and wittily, and I've got to get David into a mask and get his head
still. I'm very happy with the way Greg is working: his Servant speech today
was wonderful. But there are other things I don't know about yet. I'm a little
worried about just the plain narrative: will the audience understand exactly
what's going on? I think they will, I hope they will. It's a kind of obsession of
mine, if they won't understand the story they won't understand anything. It's
a pretty basic need, a security you've got to give them.

Tuesday 16 April

Rehearsal room 4, the smallest one in the National, ideal for working on fine
detail. The focus today is on the scene in which the Guard brings the disguised
Dionysus in to Pentheus as his prisoner.

David is testing out the Guard's state of mind, and his attitude to the king. "It's
rather brave of him to tell him about the women escaping, isn't it?" he muses.
"But actually it's a military report; that's how I shall think of it." Peter
encourages him: "Yes, you're having to tell him elliptically, because these are
supernatural events. But it's important that you switch us in to your anxieties."
They do the scene again, but after further interruptions for discussion Peter
says: "Let's not elaborate the incidents. The main action is that a common
soldier is saying, There's more in this than meets the eye." By the end David
has found an appropriate tone for the speech.

Back in the larger space the opening chorus has regressed since last week. The
actors voice some anxieties, mainly about over-elaboration: "It disempowers
us if we have to move too much," Jax says. Peter has put in a tricky cross-stage
movement that looks beautiful, but is causing one or two collisions. "It's the
director being desperate, wanting to give the audience something to look at,"
he admits. The move is cut. "Are we being animalistic enough?" Wendy asks.
Harry intervenes to sharpen up the Bacchic cry of "Euoi".

The afternoon sees further problems with the scene between Cadmus, Agave
and Pentheus' head. The self-pitying note has crept in again. "We're telling the
audience it's a sad, sad story, but they already know that," Peter says. Will is

having difficulties with the pulse: "When we read it it's okay, but with the mask I can't keep my belief in the pauses; as you wait you lose the impulse. I'm getting bogged down in the sound." Harry suggests speeding up the pulse, but Peter wants to keep it as it is. To Will he says: "I've got to stop blaming you, and you've got to stop blaming the pulse. You're doing some very good work, we've hit a brick wall, but it's not a crisis. Trust me."

Meanwhile he has another anxiety. "We still don't have the real masks, and that worries me. Three weeks tomorrow we meet our first audience."

— —

Wendy Morgan
The first rehearsal masks were almost featureless. They were supposed to be a cast of what you looked like, but I didn't like what I saw, so I rejected it. I'm much happier with the new mask: I don't know if it looks like me, but it's just got strong features, it looks more like a person, and I can go with that.

— —

Rebecca Lenkiewicz
'I really enjoyed the first session with the *Oedipus* masks, I felt there was a connection, I had a very good time. But I don't get a charge from the rehearsal masks. And even if I did, it would be very difficult to keep up the emotional stamina day after day. I think you'd burn yourself out before the first preview.

— —

David Ryall
It's a nice life when you get your mask, but I'm quite glad I haven't got mine yet. I know it will add something, so I don't want to get there too quickly. Part of me wants to postpone the moment, although I also want to know that it's going to be right.

Thursday 18 April
Rehearsals are becoming more assured as the work of the Chorus, principals and musicians becomes more integrated. Nikola is coming up with a powerful range of samples, which add enormously to the atmosphere. Peter is concerned about the volume of the music in the choruses, but Harry reassures him: "A lot of it is in the cracks, and we can tone it down when they speak."

Marie is rehearsing the movements for the 'Go you hounds of Hecate' chorus, which now has its full quota of Harry's fiendish, terrifying music. "Try to get a gang feeling, become more predatory," she tells the actors, and they do so. Peter reminds them that the music has to appear to be induced by the Chorus, and not the other way round. They must not *follow* the music. If they do, they are late. He also emphasises their motivation: "It only works as a group of people wanting to seduce the audience. It should be ugly but jubilant, a carnival of blood."

In the afternoon the Chorus rehearses the earthquake invoked by Dionysus, probably the most complex scene to stage. The actors sit on the ground while Harry takes them through the music, which begins with swanee whistles and ends with a cataclysmic rending sound as the stage splits. When they try it, they find it hard to pick up the cues in the exact rhythm. Two or three exchange slightly hysterical giggles when they get it wrong. "It's a bit like school," Harry says afterwards. "But it's been a hard day for them."

— —

Harrison Birtwistle
My big disappointment, and it's theirs too, is that I haven't been able to write much for the singers. There's a little, and I'm going to continue trying, but I don't think there's enough time, and I can't honestly say I can see somewhere else where there should be singing. I think probably the voices we have are too operatic. You really need folk voices, and I should have known that.

— —

Margaret Preece
What Harry has done with the band and the rhythm has been extraordinary. But I'm disappointed that there hasn't been more singing. I think a little bit more experimentation could have gone on. We were very willing.

— —

Renzo Murrone
As solo singers we had expectations, we felt there could have been more material for us. So we had a couple of weeks being very frustrated. But then we realised that it was not going to evolve, so we abandoned that idea and just got on with the play, which is great anyway. It's really coming together now, but it's a bit painstaking: repeat, repeat, repeat. So now we're just desperate to get on stage.

Friday 19 April

During the week some of the Chorus have become dispirited. They're feeling uncertain about who they are as Asian women, and unhappy about having to do so much movement work, which they feel has become too separated from the rest of the rehearsals. They're also feeling somewhat overwhelmed and confused by the demands being made on them from different directions.

This morning Peter gives them what he later calls "a team talk". On the question of motivation, he says that all they have to remember is that they're a group of actors putting on a play, and that their one aim in the choruses is to persuade both the audience and the women of Thebes to join them. He says that their hard work will be rewarded once they get on the stage, but it will continue to be tough, and if anyone feels it's all too much for them, they should consider if they would be happier if they left.

The actors seem reassured by his remarks. At the end of the day they're all still there.

– –

Cordelia Monsey
Some of the Chorus were very negative before Peter's talk, but now all the tension has gone. What is fascinating to watch is his sense of timing, how shrewd he is in his choices of what to say when, whether he's talking to an individual actor or to the whole company.

– –

Peter Hall
I'm very happy with the Chorus now. The component parts are there, more or less. The music and the pulses and the words are starting to come together, and the physical life is developing. They're not yet free in their speech, they're doing it too rhythmically and too mechanically, not yet allowing their humanity to come through. But that's the next stage. I think they're a very good group, and this week they've gelled into something that's going to work.

6. Getting There

"It's very difficult to introduce singing as if it's completely natural. I don't know if I'll manage it" – Harrison Birtwistle

Tuesday 23 April

A solid morning of drilling work on two of the choruses. The 'Hounds of Hecate' one needs most attention. Peter becomes choreographer again, moving amongst the actors, adding a grotesque finale to the re-enactment of Pentheus' death. He clarifies the shifting mood, stressing the need to keep the mocking tone, the relish of the violence. "It's zealots, it's lynch law, they're kind of nuts, they're possessed," he suggests. "Euripides is saying, How much further can they go before they realise what a dangerous cult they are endorsing?"

After lunch eight young women, dance colleagues and students of Marie, join the company. Cordelia and Steven, in conjunction with the casting department, have had the job of recruiting them. They're to play the women of Thebes whom Dionysus drives raving up the mountain. Peter shows them the set model and uses it to explain their part in the opening chorus. He and Marie then devise moves to send them up the mountain, making sure they fit in with Harry's music. As dancers the newcomers have no difficulty in facing front throughout, even without masks on. Their presence, and Peter's addition of some brief simulated sexual activity by the actors, gives the opening chorus a harder, more ecstatic tone. Peter: "It's cooking." Harry: "It's coming off the back burner."

Greg and David as Teiresias and Cadmus, looking suitably absurd with their ivy wreaths and phallic shafts, catch effectively the comic elements in their initial scene. "It's two old men who want to go to the party, but they're very inappropriately dressed." Peter suggests. He emphasises the purpose of the comedy: "It lightens the atmosphere, it gives the audience a break before it goes to the opposite extreme when Pentheus enters."
Greg observes: "There's no way we're going to get the level of comedy until we're in front of an audience and in masks." Peter agrees, and makes it known to the stage management that he's "a bit pissed off" about the final masks not yet being available.

– –

Clare Swinburne
Yesterday and today have been very helpful for all of us. Peter gave us total focus and really started to connect to the play. Last week we were very disheartened, because we felt the gulf between what we were doing and the play was massive, that movement was being put on things without us knowing why. Get up, go back, come forward, get in a clump – all that's very hard. You've got some extremely talented actors in the Chorus without any identity behind a mask in these huge shawls, and it takes a lot to be able to do all that and do your job well, knowing you're not going to get any personal recognition for it.

Thursday 25 April
"Stand by for the earthquake!" announces stage manager Ernie Hall. The scene involves Pentheus' palace being shaken to the ground. "We've set all this, but no one seems to know it, let alone me," Peter admits. It's a violent, very physical scene, that changes abruptly from joy to fear, from shock to ecstasy within a few lines. Greg demonstrates some *capoeira* moves, and the Chorus use them to whirl about in convincing fashion. "It's going to work," Peter says.

After lunch the final masks for both principals and Chorus arrive. Some have hair attached, which for the Chorus means dreadlocks. The actors exchange views animatedly. Peter wanders across: "I don't want to be pompous, but you need to treat the mask with respect, not just use it as a prop." The room falls silent, and for 20 minutes the actors work on inhabiting their masks.

Peter then asks for reactions. Lee wonders if he looks too like Bob Marley, too masculine. Greg's mask is riding up his face, and needs another fitting. But most of the actors seem happy to have their real mask at last. "And mine seems happy with me," David observes, in response to his Cadmus mask. Peter advises: "Use them as much as possible, get to know their strengths and weaknesses. If you don't feel comfortable or real, do say so, and Alison and Vicki can adjust them for you." He then initiates a series of exercises with the whole company, aimed at helping them keep their mask facing front as much of the time as possible, even when they're turning upstage. He invites them to mirror Greg who, from the front of the room, spends ten minutes taking them in slow motion through a wide range of movements, encouraging them always to work from the centre of their body.

Alison and Vicki observe their handiwork from the front, and discuss it with Peter. Suddenly a problem arises. Peter feels the Chorus masks are not eastern enough in the oriental sense, that they are Indian or Turkish. Alison says that has always been the intention, as she thought was clear from her costume designs and the casts of the faces. Peter admits he misread them. After rehearsal the three of them meet to try to solve this unexpected dilemma. They agree there are only two options: to create a batch of oriental masks from scratch, or try to make the present masks more like what Peter thought he was getting. After they've tested the colour of different masks under the lights in the rehearsal room, it's agreed that Vicki will re-paint one of the new masks and see if Peter approves. The meeting breaks up in an air of gloom.

– –

Alison Chitty
Modelling and thinking about the masks takes a long time. Even when the masks are finished, they have to go to the wig department to have the wigs attached, then to the sound department to have the mikes attached, and then to the actors to be fitted and to make sure they're all right. So when somebody last week on a difficult day said, When are we having the masks? it was a fine line whether it was better to shoot the person or shoot me. There's no way that we can know.

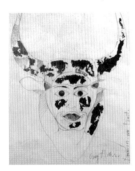  

Masks in development: drawing by Alison Chitty, masks made by Vicki Hallam

Friday 26 April
Peter has asked for a run-through, the first with the performance masks. Before it begins Greg warns him that he can't speak very well through his Dionysus mask, and may have to take it off at some point. In fact he's compelled to do so after only a dozen lines. Happily his Teiresias mask fits well, and makes him look convincingly ancient, as does David's as Cadmus. Will's Pentheus mask suggests the clean-cut, sharp young ruler, with just a hint of androgyny, while his Agave one is seriously feminine.

The run takes one hour fifty-five minutes: ten minutes still need to be lost. Peter begins his notes with an encouraging word: "I'm absolutely convinced that we can make this work to an extraordinary level, and create something amazing." He says he feels the dance and movement are now working well. While recognising that the actors are wearing their proper masks for the first time, he outlines his concerns. He says the piece is terribly slow, mainly because it's too even-paced. The principals need to move their scenes along a bit; the recognition scene requires more variety, more anger. The music is too loud, drowning out many of the words. Lines are being split in the middle, and quite a lot of the text is inaccurate. The choruses lack precision, clarity, energy. "They're still too well-bred. I don't want caution, I want danger."

— —

Harrison Birtwistle
I think we still need to make the piece musically more like itself. There's always a point when it's like tightening a nut, giving it that extra turn. I think we've invented its world, but I can't really assess the production any more in the rehearsal room. We now need to see it in the theatre.

— —

Peter Hall
There is a big problem with pace, from the arrival of the messenger to tell us of the death of Pentheus through to the end. We're dealing with shock after shock after shock, it's woe and misery and doom and gloom, and it's terribly slow. I can feel the audience all reaching for their bags in order to catch the last train home, so I'll be watching that very acutely.

Greg's lost at the moment because he hasn't got comfortable, achieved masks he can work with. It's not fair on him, and he's suffering. Will is struggling to carry on being a naturalistic actor, although he's not playing a naturalistic part or a naturalistic text, and he's got a mask on. I think he comes and goes as a consequence. I hope he'll get there, because I think he's extraordinarily talented. But I don't think he's endorsing what the play demands all the time; sometimes he's resisting it. David is an *echt* naturalistic actor and always comes to his performances extremely late. He'll do it at the last minute. They're all slightly traumatised at the moment, but I think they'll be fine.

Although there's now only a week to go before we go into the Olivier, basically we're where we should be. There are certain things that have got to be done and certain people who have to move in directions which they may find it difficult to do or not want to do. If we can do that, I think we've got something.

Tuesday 30 April

The last week in the rehearsal room. Peter aims to have several runs, but also work on the detail of certain scenes he's not yet satisfied with.

This afternoon with Greg and David he's finessing the first, occasionally comic scene between Teiresias and Cadmus. The banter between the two of them as to which is the older is a running joke. "I'm afraid it's only crawling at the moment," David confesses. Peter emphasises a key element in Teiresias' world-view: "He's unpopular with all fanatical rulers like Pentheus because he sees three sides to every question."

They look again at the wild opening Bacchic chorus. Peter wants it even harsher than before. "Suit the action to the word," he says. "Try experimenting with tearing and eating the flesh when you get to the still living mountain goat.' They do so with relish. "That was pretty hairy, very good, I knew what you were about that time."

The ivy-covered shafts, overtly phallic, provoke the odd moment of ribaldry. Peter asks for them to be used in a more overtly sexual manner. "Don't be shy, ladies, hold them up more vertically." Rachel: "I was thinking of using mine as a weapon." Peter: "I don't mind that, as long as they're erect." Someone asks him if they should bang them on the floor at one point. "Ask Harry, that's the aural department," he replies. But Harry is worried about creating a Morris dancers image. After they try it he decides it's more like Snow White and the Seven Dwarfs.

The 'Sweet river' chorus, the most lyrical one, is causing some trouble; Peter feels it has several "dead" moments. He reminds them of the story they are telling, and as they do it again he gestures with both hands and face to emphasise the emotions. "That's a knockout," he announces. "There's a fantastic emotional energy developing. You're getting too big for this room."

After normal rehearsals end, Steve carries on with the sessions he's been having all week with the understudies, all of whom are drawn from the Chorus. This evening he's working on the recognition scene, with Rebecca as Agave, Geoffrey as Cadmus, and Nicola reading the Chorus' lines. At this stage he's concentrating on technical matters, on getting the breathing and stresses right. Rebecca quickly catches the fierce ecstasy of Agave, while Geoffrey, despite his relative youth, seems set to make an authoritative Cadmus.

– –

Will Houston
Once you iron out the moments that aren't working, you feel able to relax more, have longer periods when you can be in character, and not be thinking, Oh my God, I haven't got this bit right, what am I going to do? Then you can keep running it, begin to form your journey, and let go of your third eye that's always monitoring and checking what you're doing. But I think we're going to need balls of steel for the previews, because I don't think we're going to be as close as many of us would like to be to getting it right. So we're still going to have to experiment and fail in front of an audience.

– –

Greg Hicks
'Teiresias I know about, I like the mask a lot. With the Servant, it's just a question of putting his long speech into the mask – I've only done it twice so far. But the Dionysian priest remains a conundrum. I'm trying to find my way into the mask, but my relationship with him is not comfortable yet. There's a quality I can't catch, something to do with an absolute child-like openness – I keep hearing myself being quite sardonic and slightly knowing. But I have a feeling I'll find the way I'm going to do it during the previews.

Thursday 2 May
The fine tuning continues, in preparation for a run this afternoon. Peter is still pushing the Chorus to anticipate their words with yet more precision; just one or two seconds' pause and the momentum is lost. Harry observes of the 'Soon shall we know again' chorus: "The other day you caught it with great intensity and energy without the music. Try and find that again."

As they work the principals' masks are being brought in by Vicki. Dionysus' bull mask is a large, potent and glittering gold head. The mask that fits underneath is being worked on: Peter finds it "too predatory and smart, whereas the point about the priest is that he is the most trustworthy and open-faced naïve sweet young man".

It's now Peter's turn to be off the book. For this run he finally abandons the script and his pen for the first time, and simply watches and listens. What he sees pleases him. "That was definitely another notch up. The Chorus worked brilliantly, their journey was very clear." But he still wants them to slow the physical side down. "When the masks are on, the very slightest movement is effective," he reminds them.

In the early evening Steve and Cordelia work with a dozen men, the "supernumeraries", who are to play Pentheus' guard. Machine guns are handed round, and the actors given numbers, since they are to be broken into two groups in order to alternate performances. "Try and get a pack awareness," Cordelia says. Their efforts are slightly hampered by the confines of the rehearsal room, which make their aggressive entrances difficult to rehearse.

– –

Harrison Birtwistle
The improvised material the musicians have injected into it has really developed the production, and I think it's become a very fine-tuned machine. Unless we suddenly find a few little corners, I've written all the music I'm going to write. There are a lot of things I could still do, lots of ways it could still go, but finally you come up against a brick wall, which is the performance. To add anything more now would be very difficult, the whole thing might just collapse like a pack of cards. Compared with what I normally do, these rhythms are very primitive, very simple; they couldn't be anything else. I know how to make this more complex, but there wouldn't be any point, because you've got to hear the text.

Friday 3 May
Peter spends most of the morning working with Will and David on the problematic recognition scene. "We need to be very careful with these end of the play beats," he tells the two actors. He reiterates his belief that Euripides is deliberately subverting convention. Traditionally the Greeks kept bloody actions off-stage – "But here he brings on a head and says, 'Laugh you fuckers, I'm breaking the rules.' I'm absolutely convinced it's black comedy."

After experimenting further, Will and David sit on the ground, the bloody head between them, still trying to pin down the emotional logic of the scene. Peter is emphatic: "It mustn't be sentimental, you have to play it as if you're keeping the tears at bay." David assents: "Yes, the more factual, the more moving."

The Chorus then have one final go at the opening, this time without masks. It's now developed a powerful sexual charge. "I love it," Peter says. "The concentration is enormous." Harry too is very satisfied. "It was like a coiled spring," he remarks. Colin wonders whether the Chorus should all say the key word in the line "Where the God *pricks* the women wild". Harry: "No, I think one prick at a time."

For the final run Peter, Harry and Colin have invited a handful of friends in to watch, including Bill Mason, Director of the Chicago Lyric Opera, and his wife. "Tell the story to them," he suggests. "But remember this run is more for you than for us." Before they start the Chorus make a tight circle, arms on each other's shoulders, for a breathing exercise which Patsy has taught them. They and the principals then run the play with increasing confidence, style and precision, chopping two minutes off the running time.

Peter is satisfied: "Just the run we wanted. We're now ready for the stage." He refrains from giving detailed notes at this moment. Instead Ernie runs through the schedule for the technical rehearsal, which begins tomorrow evening, continues for ten hours each day on Monday and Tuesday, with a dress rehearsal on Tuesday evening and another on Wednesday afternoon, before the first preview that evening. Angie then announces the schedule for the final mask and costume fittings.

Peter concludes: "Being in costume, full body make-up and masks for three days is going to be hellish. I suggest you spend tomorrow afternoon in bed." Afterwards the actors stay on chatting longer than usual, as if reluctant to leave the place where so much has been created. In fact they're now raring to get on stage.

– –

David Ryall
I love to have people watching, it gives you a lift, it reminds you what you're playing for. Rehearsing for nine weeks playing it to Peter is a bit like having a driving instructor: you eventually feel the need to push off on your own.

– –

Peter Hall
In its passion and intent I thought the run-through was good enough to warrant the move to the stage. We now need to edit out everything that is decorative or unnecessary or confusing. Harry has unleashed his musicians at full tilt, so the problem of making the words clear and balancing them in volume with the music is going to be one of the main tasks in the technical rehearsal. The other big one will be the lighting. With the set being a huge wooden disc, the visual interest will be the patterns the Chorus make on the stage. This probably means an infinite number of extremely subtle and almost unnoticeable lighting cues, moving from one to another, which can only be done with the Chorus there, in their masks and in their costumes.

Normally in lighting rehearsals you have an assistant stage manager or somebody walking the actors' parts. But you can't have fifteen people walking the Chorus, it's too much to contemplate. So the lighting plot is going to be very, very difficult.

7. Into the Olivier

"I'm frightened but confident" – Peter Hall

Saturday 4 May
7 o'clock in the evening. The last lap of the journey. The actors are finally on stage, in full costume, with the correct masks, ready for the technical rehearsal to begin. The set could not be simpler: a vast, steeply raked, empty wooden disc, with a slender walkway rising gradually across the back from stage right to left, representing the route to the mountain.

In the centre of the stalls the lighting designer Peter Mumford and his assistant Danny Cunnett sit behind three large lighting desks. Peter Hall is next to them, ready to mastermind the rehearsal through a microphone. Harry, Alison, Carrie and Vicki are seated behind him; Paul Groothuis is on the sound desk near the back exit; the musicians, conducted by Kawai, are tucked behind the disc upstage left, beneath the walkway.

"This is one of those shows that has a pitfall every thirty seconds," Peter warns. Initial progress is certainly slow. Peter Mumford experiments with different lights, seeing what meets with Peter's approval. "I think we should underlight the Chorus, and make the others very crisp," Peter suggests. The visual effect of their red saris and fawn animal skins under the lights is stunning.

Getting the Chorus on stage without their being seen proves a major difficulty. Another is to get the right shadowy effect on the statue of Semele, which is posed by one of the mountain women. A serious worry is Greg's continuing problem putting on his bull's-head mask at the start. Much time is also spent finding the appropriate light to silhouette the women of Thebes as they move up to the mountain, casting their clothes off as they go. Finally the Chorus launch into 'Go, you Bacchai, go!' The delivery is ragged, as the actors struggle to adjust to the unfamiliar floor.

Ernie, who is responsible for keeping the rehearsal moving, is in contact through headphones with his stage management team: Angie in the cue box, Gemma and Paul backstage. Cordelia, also on "cans", moves frequently between the auditorium and the stage, acting as a go-between for Peter and the actors. Communication is often problematic, especially between the musicians and the stalls: the vastness of the Olivier now makes the rehearsal room seem positively intimate.

By the end of the evening only seven of the 60 pages of script have been covered. But Peter is reasonably content: "Not too bad for a first shot."

— —

Jax Williams
I was worried at first, it was so incredibly slow. The original concept seemed so simple, I just thought, What's going on? I was totally disoriented by the space, and suddenly hearing the music come from different parts of the auditorium, and having the mike pack weighing down on the back of my neck, and dealing with the heavier raw silk wraps. But now I'm starting to enjoy it, it's a very alive space, and with the rake you feel more immediately open to the audience, which is great.

— —

Peter Mumford
Although we're working on a bare stage, it's quite a complex show to light, because the lighting has to fulfil both a narrative and a pictorial role. Because the actors are the main scenic element, we're lighting it as we might light a contemporary dance piece. We've gone down quite an expressionist road, using very bold colour, and I think that's working. Peter is very open to ideas, very receptive to what I've been throwing at him. He seems to be really enjoying the use of colour.

Monday 6 May

10.30 am. As the rehearsal continues the costumes of the principals are gradually revealed for all to see. Offsetting the deep-red saris of the Asian women, Teiresias and Cadmus are decked out in cream tropical suits, while Pentheus is dressed in a long, blue-grey military coat with gold braid on his shoulders. His soldiers, in boiler-suit uniforms and threatening visors, seem almost like a second Chorus. The wooden stage, now being enhanced by some exquisite lighting ideas, shows off the strong colours to brilliant effect. "The basic lighting language is a knockout," Peter observes.

Some of the masks are in need of tweaking, either technical or physical. Vicki moves on and off stage making the necessary adjustments, cutting the pieces of foam inside the mask to bring it nearer to the face, or making a mouth slightly bigger. Peter is happy with most of the masks, though not yet sure about David's one for Cadmus: "I think he needs more natural dignity, it makes him look too much like a silly old codger," he tells Alison.

The length of the saris is causing difficulties for some of the actors: Alison agrees to shorten them by about a foot during the tea break, to help their movement. Meanwhile Peter decides to cut the soldiers' guns: "They're like a strident sub-text, a slogan saying these men are real and dangerous and Pentheus is a fascist," he says. "The uniforms and visors do that; the guns overstate it.' But the balance between the volume of the music and the words the Chorus speak is now much improved; only the occasional phrase is drowned out by a flourish of woodwind or the beating of a drum. Even now Peter ("I don't want to wallpaper, but...") is asking for some tiny additions to the sound, "a little touch of Harry" here and there.

Considering the complexity of the show, the atmosphere is remarkably calm. The actors are coping patiently with the regular stops and starts, and the inevitable fragmentation of their performances they cause. The Chorus are gradually adjusting their movements to the unfamiliar rake. But progress is still very slow. At lunch Peter admits there's no hope of getting a dress-rehearsal tomorrow night, as he had hoped. However, towards the end of the evening he stages a run of the 25 pages they've covered so far. Though it includes the complicated earthquake, it goes impressively smoothly. So the actors leave at eleven on a high note.

— —

Greg Hicks
I feel the work is coming together rather well. Quite what people will make of it I don't know: I think they'll either love it or hate it. They certainly won't be indifferent to it. I fall in and out of love with it. I look at it one day and think, We've really got this right, then I look again the next and think, God, we've got this all wrong.

— —

David Ryall
In the rehearsal room we had the mask absolutely out front. In fact Greek audiences watched the play from almost three sides, and I think here on this circular set you can share the mask round a little. It means you can at least get a glimpse of the other actors, which is a great relief.

— —

William Houston
Often in the technical you find you've got half an hour when you're standing

on the stage while the lighting is being fixed, and you can just practise something for a little bit in a way you wouldn't dare to do normally unless the director was with you. So it's a brilliant time for me.

Tuesday 7 May

11.00 am. Day 3 of the technical starts on a farcical note: the showers are not working, which makes it very difficult for the Chorus to be able to wash off their all-over body make-up. To help Peter Mumford with his lighting decisions, two of the actors agree to put it on anyway.

The characters' entrances invariably take up a disproportionate amount of time, with music and lighting cues needing to be timed to precision. This morning the sticking-point is David's entry as the Herdsman. Timing his positioning for his opening lines as he descends proves difficult; his rustic crook gets stuck between the boards; and the steps on to the stage prove almost impossible to negotiate in shadow wearing a mask. Finally it's agreed that the music will be extended slightly to give him more time. "Harry will write you a Pastoral Symphony to fill the gap," Peter tells him.

The actors' microphones still cause trouble now and then. At one point a debate takes place between Peter, Harry and Paul about the causes of inaudibility in the 'Go, hounds of Hecate' chorus. Paul believes the actors are losing clarity because they are shouting, and wonders if the music should have less volume. But Peter feels the grotesqueness of the chorus requires the music to be at a high level, so he asks the actors to speak louder, but to avoid shouting.

During a break a photographer arrives to take pictures of Peter and Harry for the *Evening Standard*. When he expresses surprise at finding "an empty stage", Harry explains: "It's not the plate that counts, it's the food that's on it."

In the afternoon Agave's arrival with her son's head uncovers problems in the recognition scene. Will asks for some rubber to be put on the base of his stockings to prevent his slipping when he runs down the walkway. He's also worried about the weight of the head, and the fact that it rotates on the shaft. From both the stalls and the back of the circle the production looks visually stunning. The combination of subtle lighting and savage music for the choruses produces an effect at once barbaric and beautiful. Already the actors have gained hugely in confidence and sure-footedness, and the weeks of insistent drilling on both words and movement are starting to pay off handsomely.

But in the evening there's a major problem. For Dionysus' final appearance Greg is supposed to rise through the floor on a small circular platform. This is a potentially dangerous manoeuvre anyway: there's a forty-foot drop immediately below him, and his safety has to be assured. But the machinery doesn't move fast enough for his cue. Other options are tried, until it's decided he should come on stage hiding behind the shroud used to cover Pentheus' bones, and then emerge from under it. The snag here is that he can be seen from the circle and the side stalls. After two hours of experimenting tempers are getting frayed, and there's no solution in sight. Peter calls an extra rehearsal for the morning to try to solve the problem, and to run the mechanically complex earthquake once more.

– –

Harrison Birtwistle
When you get into another space it always brings up problems. But this is only fine-tuning now as far as the sound goes. I thought it was a bit soggy initially, but we'll get it right. Overall a lot of things have come up in these nine weeks that I hadn't planned. But fundamentally it's what I thought it would be – only better.

– –

Alison Chitty
I feel very thrilled about the nature of the stage, how that great sweep holds the Olivier. I love the relationship of the great disc to the auditorium in the stalls, but also the way lifting the actors in the space gives them such a fantastic relationship with people in the circle. I also think the masks, which have been very complicated, are getting better all the time as we make some final adjustments; it's going to be fascinating to see how the audience responds to them. But I'm nervous about the costumes of the Asian women. I'm pleased that we've got a very fine suede and such a beautiful colour for their animal skins, but it's a bit frightening wondering whether we've avoided the Asterix in Gaul look.

– –

Peter Hall
It's very hard to create a world in which the Greek character can exist in a modern way, but I think we've achieved it. The saris and the dreadlocks, a brilliant stroke of Alison's, constantly remind the audience both of the antique and the modern. But I have my eye on several things I may cut, such as the number of lighting cues, and the Theban women going up the mountain more than once – I think I'm over-illustrating that. Essentially it all

needs to be pared down during the previews. I won't say I do most of my work then, but I do an enormous amount. That's not to say what we offer the public before the opening will be ill-considered. It just won't be *finally* considered.

Wednesday 8 May

11.00 am. The earthquake works pretty smoothly, with only one or two minor anxieties. Even with the Chorus unmasked and in their day clothes, the effect is spectacular and thrilling.

Peter – "I'm reminded of my fifty-year resolution not to rely on stage machinery' – has decided to go for the shroud option for Dionysus' last entry. But it still takes time to make sure Greg is hidden properly. His obvious frustration is increased when his bull's horns get tangled in the shroud, and his mike pack presses into him when he lies down. "This is driving me nuts," he says. Peter promises him that an alternative mask is now being made as a fallback.

Greg still has to use the platform once he's on stage, so the remaining time is spent coordinating its rise and fall with the text. At the first attempt Will has to say his last few lines at breakneck speed to ensure Greg is still visible for his last one. Finally, Dionysus vanishes through the floor with perfect timing.

3.00 pm. Groups of people are dotted round the stage, checking last-minute details before the dress-rehearsal begins. Peter has moved out from behind the lighting desk so he has a clear view of the stage, with Cordelia behind him, poised to take notes. A smattering of National staff and friends provide an audience for the actors to play to. The stage gradually clears, stillness descends. The actors are at last ready to put together the fragmented pieces of the last three days.

The performance throws up several problems, some technical, some human. The earthquake and Dionysus episodes pass muster, but there are ragged moments with the volume of the sound, and several uncertain or mistimed music and lighting cues. David has to remove his Cadmus mask for a few lines, as he feels it's suffocating him. There is only one stoppage, when the Herdsman fails to materialise on cue. Ernie steps on stage to announce that he's on his way (he's actually in the lift). When he appears David acknowledges his lapse, in character: "I've come *nearly* directly from Mount Cithairon," he tells Pentheus.

– –

Peter Hall
We got through it, and nobody got killed. There were lots of mistakes, lots of technical problems. I would be happier if we had another day's work before we had an audience, because it's not ready. I wouldn't like to be the actors having to do it. Confidence is a very fragile thing, and they don't actually know – and neither do I – how the audience is going to take a lot of it, whether they will accept it or be totally mystified by it. The big question is, are we clear enough, are we confident enough, is the balance of the music to the words good enough, is the lighting good enough for us to actually tell the story? If we can do that, we'll be all right. But I doubt we will do it tonight.

5.00 pm. Peter receives a message telling him that the supernumeraries cannot be called for rehearsal from here on. They are not actors, so Equity rules say they can be *placed*, but not rehearsed. He is not pleased. "It means we can't solve the problem of whether or not Greg comes up, goes down, or is in a shroud. It's one of the instances where bureaucracy buggers art. The front office don't know what the supers do, that it's a matter of safety, and the courage of the leading actor. The timing is exquisite in its stupidity."

7.15 pm. An empty space, a bull's-head mask, and a nearly full house. Dionysus enters with the house lights still on, to start "the transformation from the humdrum to the wild abandon of the play". Greg dons his glittering mask without a hitch: "So let us play, so let us beat the drum...' The house lights dim, the play begins.

The contrast with the dress rehearsal is startling. The principal actors are newly confident and relaxed, the mask lessons have been learned, and they perform their lengthy speeches with great narrative drive, variety and intensity. The Chorus, enhanced by the bold and beautiful lighting, have become a tightly knit group, displaying true Bacchic power and sensuality in word and movement. The music is sharper, clearer, better defined in its blend of savagery and lyricism. The technical side works well, with Greg just managing to find his feet on the platform before it rises ten feet in the air at the play's climax.

The audience are noticeably held throughout. The story has been told.

Bacchai opened on Friday 17 May. Jonathan Croall's account of the first night, the play's reception, and the staging of the play in Epidaurus in Greece at the end of June can be found on www.nationaltheatre.org.uk/publications from early July.

"Look, and you'll begin to see." Greg Hicks as Dionysus

"Since when have you nurtured such desires?" Greg Hicks as Dionysus, William Houston as Pentheus

PHOTOGRAPHS BY MANUEL HARLAN

"Look at him who does not respect the gods." The Chorus

Above: "I seem to see two suns in the sky." William Houston as Pentheus, Greg Hicks as Dionysus

Right: "I too intend to dance." David Ryall as Cadmus, Greg Hicks as Teiresias

The following books, CDs and videos relating to *Bacchai* and Greek drama are on sale from the National's Bookshop – 020 7452 3456 or bookshop@nationaltheatre.org.uk. Secure online ordering: www.nationaltheatre.org

Playtexts

Bacchai by Euripides, in a new translation by Colin Teevan (Oberon Books, 2002)
Iph.... by Colin Teevan, from Euripides' *Iphigenia in Aulis* (Oberon Books)
Tantalus by John Barton, with additional text by Colin Teevan. (Oberon Books)
There are numerous other versions of *Bacchai* and other Greek plays available.

Books

Exposed by the Mask (including 'The Greek Stage') by Peter Hall (Oberon Books)
Making an Exhibition of Myself: The Autobiography of Peter Hall (Oberon Books)
Power Play: The Life and Times of Peter Hall by Stephen Fay (Hodder and Stoughton)

Cambridge Companion to Greek Tragedy edited by P E Easterling (CUP)
Greek Theatre Performance by David Wiles (CUP)
Tragedy in Athens: Performance Space and Theatrical Meaning by David Wiles (CUP)
Reading Greek Tragedy by Simon Goldhill (CUP)
Greek Tragedy: An Introduction by Marion Baldock (Duckworth)
Radical Theatre: Greek Tragedy and the Modern World by Rush Rehm (Duckworth)
Rape in Antiquity: Sexual Violence in the Greek and Roman Worlds edited
by Susan Deacy and Karen F. Pierce (Duckworth)
Surviving Greek Tragedy by Robert Garland [October 2002](Duckworth)
A Visitor's Guide to Greek Drama or Oedipus Who?: A Very Fractured Review
by Vernon Vas Elliot (Efstathiadis Group)
Look Inside: a Greek Theatre by Peter Chrisp (Hodder Wayland)
The Eating of the Gods; an Interpretation of Greek Tragedy
by Jan Kott and Boleslaw Taborski (Northwestern University Press)
Tragedy and the Tragic: Greek Theatre and Beyond edited by M S Silk (OUP)
Literature in the Greek World edited by Oliver Taplin
Revenge Tragedy: Aeschylus to Armageddon by John Kerrigan (OUP)
Greek Tragic Theatre by Rush Rehm (Routledge)
Greek Drama and Dramatists by Alan H. Sommerstein (Routledge)
Theatre in Ancient Greek Society by J R Green (Routledge)
The Greek Sense of Theatre: Tragedy Reviewed by J Michael Walton
Comic Angels (Approaches to Greek Drama Through Vase-Painting) by Oliver Taplin (OUP)
Ancient Greek Literature by Kenneth Dover and Others (OUP)
The Birth of Tragedy by Friedrich Nietzsche (OUP)
Dionysiac Poetics and Euripides' Bacchae by Charles Segal (Princeton University Press)

Videos

Oedipus Rex Film by Pier Paulo Pasolini, inspired by Sophocles
Medea Film by Pier Paulo Pasolini from Euripides

CDs

Oedipus by Sophocles (Naxos Audiobooks – also on audiocassette)
For news of a possible recording of the choruses from the NT production of *Bacchai*, music by
Harrison Birtwistle, visit nationaltheatre.org.uk/backstage/music

Also the programme for Peter Hall's National Theatre production of *Bacchai*, with specially
commissioned articles by Colin Teevan and Edith Hall, a selection of gift items and a
comprehensive range of playtexts, books on theatre history, biographies and books on technique.

Availability may be subject to change.